Matheson

TO THE TOP:

A PERSONAL BEST APPROACH TO SUCCESS

Anthony M. Stewart

PORT
CAMPBELL
PRESS

Port Campbell Press
25 Colonial Drive, Vermont South, Victoria 3133

Edited by Wendy Skilbeck
Designed by Jo Waite Design
Production management by Greenglades Publishing Services
Typeset in Centennial by J&M Typesetting
Printed in Australia by Printgraphics Pty Ltd

National Library of Australia
cataloguing-in-publication data:

Stewart, Anthony M.
  To the top: a personal best approach to success.

  ISBN 0 646 24072 2.

  1. Achievement motivation. 2. Success. 3. Leadership.
  I. Title.

158.1

FOREWORD

The critical importance of mental skills is now being recognised more than ever by those who earnestly seek success. Realisation of the relationship between psychology and performance is becoming increasingly clear. In short, it is now well documented that mental skills, involving elements such as goal setting, concentration, remaining positive, visualisation and stress control, are significant factors in controlling and optimising one's potential. Individuals everywhere are being called upon to recognise and reach their 'personal bests' so that they can climb to the top in their respective fields.

A 35-year association with committed people in learning institutions, sporting disciplines and business organisations has convinced me that psychology holds the key to most top performances.

To The Top, I believe, sets out a well-structured blueprint for your personal success through the accomplishment of individually set goals and a daily commitment to do your 'personal best' in every endeavour.

I have worked professionally with Anthony Stewart for a number of years and have utilised his no-nonsense approach and advice extensively. It has been well documented that his input has assisted elite sporting figures and successful business people in a variety of settings. Knowing his passion for his discipline I felt that it would only be a matter of time before he published another practical and informative text sharing his ideas and experiences.

To The Top provides an easily understood guide to optimising personal potential. It also gives the reader practical strategies which can be utilised immediately to enhance performance.

I would whole-heartedly recommend this book to those with ambition who have chosen to set demanding goals in their quest for the successful completion of the journey 'to the top'.

David Parkin
AFL Premiership Coach
Lecturer, Human Movement,
Deakin University

DEDICATION

I dedicate this book to those who:
- are prepared to adventure beyond known horizons and struggle against great odds in order to record great victories
- find what they want to do, and do it
- combine their dream with a pure determination to accomplish great things no matter whoever or whatever stands in their way
- radiate a strong spirit and drive to become the best in their chosen field.

CONTENTS

PREFACE

I am privileged that my professional work affords me the opportunity of working with many gifted individuals who excel in sport and business. It is my experience that successful people invariably employ a variety of mental skills in their quest to make it 'to the top'. They all understand the power of the mind and utilise techniques such as goal/target setting, remaining optimistic and positive, creative visualisation and stress control to optimise their potential. Those committed to being successful also recognise that psychology holds the key to most consistent, impressive performances.

This book is designed to encourage you to take charge of your career, sporting future—your life. Each chapter provides very practical, workable suggestions, quotes and check-lists as well as comments from very successful people. It is my hope that as a result of reading *To The Top* you will realise that you possess or can acquire the skills necessary to handle whatever challenges that may be forthcoming.

I believe that everything recommended in this book will prove worthwhile. I am confident that if you implement the concepts discussed in this book your achievement levels will undoubtedly improve. I urge you to commit yourself to practise the suggestions daily so that you become someone who is both extremely accomplished and quietly confident in your capacity to achieve whatever goals you desire.

Anthony M. Stewart

ACKNOWLEDGEMENTS

I sincerely wish to thank:
- Ray Allsopp for his assistance with the original manuscript
- Anne Forsyth, Sharleen Forsyth, Maureen Carr, Allison Carr for typing the manuscript
- Open Spaces Photography and Sporting Pix for permission to use the included photos
- My family and friends for their constant support
- Dennis Jones, Lesley Thwaites, Jo Waite and Wendy Skilbeck for the production of this book
- Pratt Paper for their support
- All the sports people who contributed their comments so willingly:

Emma Carney, World Champion Triathlete
Clare Carney, Junior World Champion Triathlete
Alwyn Barrett, Satellite Coach of the Australian Institute of Sport
Sue Stanley, World Aerobics Champion
Gary Neiwand, Triple Commonwealth Gold Cycling Sprint Champion
David Parkin, Multiple AFL Premiership Coach
Joyce Brown, OAM, Retired Australian Netball Coach
Stephen Moneghetti, Olympic and International Distance Runner
Shelley Gorman, Australian 'Opals' Basketballer
Jay Stacy, Australian Hockey Player
Anne Currie, Retired World Champion Amputee Swimmer
Jill McIntosh, National Netball Coach
Les Stillman, Victorian Cricket Team Coach
Michelle Fielke, OAM, Captain Australian Netball Team
Phil Dale, Waverley Reds Baseball Team
David Graham, Geelong Supercats Basketballer
Andrew Collins, Champion Footballer with Hawthorn in the AFL
Tammy Van Wisse, Marathon Swimming Champion
Andrew Gaze, International and Australian Basketball Player
Simone McKinnis, OAM, Australian Netball Player
Greg Williams, Champion Carlton Footballer in the AFL
Kathy Watt, Olympic and World Champion Cyclist

Alan Joyce, Dual AFL Premiership Coach

Cathy Freeman, Commonwealth and Australian Athletics Champion

Jason Dunstall, Champion Footballer and Captain of the Hawthorn
Football Club in the AFL

Paul Wade, Captain of Australian Socceroos

Lindsay Gaze, Australian and International Basketball Coach

David Wansbrough, Australian Hockey Player

Stephen Kernahan, Captain of Carlton Football Club in the AFL

Brian McNicholl, World Champion Paralympic Weight-lifter

Frances Murphy, Victorian Surf Swimming Champion

Gary Pert, Champion Footballer with Collingwood in the AFL

Michele Timms, Australian 'Opals' Basketballer

Vicki Wilson, OAM, Australian Netball Player

Robyn Maher, Australian 'Opals' Basketball Captain

Kieren Perkins, OAM, World Champion Swimmer

- Adrian Carr, Greg Buck, Leo Stewart, Don Blackwood and Diane
  Linard for reviewing the manuscript and for their constructive
  comments.

INTRODUCTION

Mental powers are essential if you wish to lift your performance levels to new heights on a consistent basis. Most individuals can perform much better than what they are currently. However, too few people understand and appreciate this fact and rather than opening doors to improved performance, wallow in frustration and disappointment.

The better performers know how to tap their pools of physical skills and vast mental strengths and waste no opportunity to display their talent. Such individuals lift themselves to consistently higher levels and daily challenge themselves to learn new skills and welcome new ideas. They accept that their rates of improvement are determined primarily by the limits imposed by themselves or other influential people.

1 Accept responsibility for your career, hitch a ride on the road to true success by appreciating that your potential is boundless and the only limit to how far you go is *how far you think you can go!* Ultimately, what you expect to happen, usually does happen.

2 Appreciate that you have unlimited potential and remove any self-imposed limitations on your performance level. Believe strongly inside that you are capable of much more and set forth on exciting new journeys of physical and mental development. Ignite your desire to confidently and continually test yourself—to tread new paths. Realise that ultimately how successful you become in any endeavour is in your own hands.

3 Take charge of your life. Accept responsibility to work hard and plan how to accomplish your dreams. Welcome help and guidance from those you trust and overcome whatever setbacks or disappointments you encounter with a burning desire to constantly improve yourself.

4 Challenge yourself daily by establishing an ongoing expectation that the maximum effort today will serve to be the minimum

■ *Remember — in life, in sport, in career, where you go and how far you go is all up to YOU!*

benchmark for tomorrow. Never underestimate the value of achieving successive small goals/targets for your self-confidence and personal development.

THE PERSONAL BEST APPROACH— PUTTING THE BEYOND WITHIN REACH

Overcoming the endless series of tiny hurdles and maximising your performance by mastering each self-improvement challenge is the true meaning of winning. Countless successful people continually lift their performance levels by pursuing a series of personal bests. Rather than being preoccupied with coming first every time, such people recognise that winning is related to confronting each problem and overcoming it. They believe that they win when they are better today than what they were yesterday—it is a quest conducted within yourself and against yourself in order to be a better self.

The personal best approach reflects that individuals are not static identities but rather are changeable, trainable and modifiable. By attempting to go beyond your personal best you will become the best possible person you can be and it might also mean that you win more than your share of contests as well.

Highly successful individuals recognise that the greatest barrier to the pursuit of excellence is not physical, that is skill and fitness, but mental, the mental barrier that inhibits the expression of the physical attributes of the performer. Champions understand that they are not going to improve or perform anywhere near full potential unless they are clear in their minds about:

i   *WHAT* THEY WISH TO ACHIEVE.
ii *HOW* THEY PLAN TO ACCOMPLISH THEIR WISHES.
iii *WHEN* THEY WISH TO ACQUIRE THIS.
iv *THE PRICE* OR SACRIFICE WILLING TO BE PAID.

Strength of mind provides the ability to overcome obstacles. This ensures that tasks are accomplished despite them once being considered impossible. Successful people develop the necessary mental approach that enables fluid expression and release of their tremendous talents. They regularly practise the techniques discussed in this book and approach mental skills as they would other skills knowing that many hours of practice are required if any realistic and measurable benefit is to be gained. Champion performers recognise that mental skills equip them to productively analyse their performance and develop a strategy that will provide them with 'the edge' over their rivals. Such skills enable these competitors to ensure all avenues available are analysed. In such conditions, pleasing performances, even personal bests, become far more common place.

■ *Remember—by striving to do your personal best you're a winner every time!*

WHAT IS THE PERSONAL BEST MENTALITY?

The personal best mentality is a state of mind concerning attitude and responsibility that enables you to express or produce your skills correctly and successfully. All consistently successful individuals exhibit this state of mind. It consists of the following qualities (give yourself a score out of ten):

Self-responsibility: A willingness to dedicate yourself to achieve the desired result. Acceptance that personal, sporting or career destiny is ultimately determined by your own daily actions and behaviour choices. There are no excuses. It is all your doing. It is all in your hands.

Self-image: The possession of an unwavering yet realistic self-belief in your capabilities.

Motivation: A relentless desire and determination to do whatever is necessary to make the maximum use of your talents.

Confidence: An unshakeable confidence derived from a positive, enthusiastic and optimistic personality concentrating on success and what can positively happen.

Mental toughness: An inner calmness and a feeling of relaxation. This allows logical thought processes to flow, producing a feeling of always being fully focussed on the job at hand and always in control, especially in stressful situations.

■ *Remember—the mind is like a parachute, it works best when it's open. Always remain open to new discoveries.*

MENTAL SKILLS FOR THE PB MENTALITY (FEELING)

  i   Relaxation
  ii Goal setting
 iii Visualisation
 iv Concentration
  v   Communication

You will learn how to apply all these skills as you proceed through the book.

SUCCESS

High-achieving individuals understand that there are no short cuts to success. Hard work is what makes their dreams come true. Those who experience success do so because they discipline themselves, make daily sacrifices and work tirelessly to achieve their goals. Champions make a daily commitment to improvement and

The 10 Cs of

SUCCESS

Calm
Confident
Cooperative
Communication
Concise skill execution
Concentration
Community minded
Creative
Control
Courage

consciously work harder than their opponents to establish an advantage—commonly referred to as 'the edge'.

Universally, successful people radiate an inner, realistic belief in themselves and transmit positive, encouraging qualities to whomever they meet. They enjoy what they do and think in terms of challenges. They are people of quality who refuse to quit when the going gets tough.

Genuinely successful individuals live with strong purpose and display a character that demands respect from their opponents. They are self-honest, loyal, respect others and will never compromise on what they know is right.

Kieren Perkins, Greg Norman and Carl Lewis

World champion performers Kieren Perkins, Greg Norman and Carl Lewis are high-achieving individuals who radiate the qualities essential for consistent success. Perkins places no limits on himself and is renowned for maintaining an enormous training load whilst preparing to establish new world records. Greg Norman, 'The Shark', remains one of the most consistent elite performers in any sport. His immense skill and inner confidence combined with 6 to 8 hours on the practice fairway hitting 800 balls a day ensures that he remains amongst the top group of world golfers.

Eight-time Olympic gold medallist Carl Lewis continually radiates the desire to win and the desire to compete at the highest level. His perseverance and self-discipline over 16 years of track and field athletics remains an inspiration to all who strive for personal excellence.

Kieren Perkins, Greg Norman and Carl Lewis are all examples of individuals who, whilst exceptionally talented, dedicate themselves to accomplishing their dreams via a daily commitment to self-improvement. They constantly demonstrate a genuine commitment to reaching their highest level of performance and strive to remain at that level consistently.

Hard work is what makes their dreams come true.

CHAPTER 1

SUCCESS: A PERSONAL BEST APPROACH

Doing better today than you did yesterday

So you want to be successful? Or, in terms of our definition of success as outlined in the introduction, you want to develop the 'personal best mentality'. What then needs to be done? What do you do to become successful? Answers are provided by studying the qualities and characteristics of proven successful individuals. We will do this in this chapter. You can then discover which of these qualities you need to develop further and thus develop your own personal best mentality. A personal best mentality can only be developed with a personal best approach.

WHAT IS SUCCESS?

Success is the ability to consistently produce personal best performances, i.e. to do better today than you did yesterday.

Always think of success this way—achieving PBs.

It's a terrific system.

1 Everybody can do it, no matter what level of sport or business they are involved in.
2 Concentrated and well-planned attacks on PBs over a period of time can take you to the top of your level, even into higher levels, and even to the top of the tree. Success really has no limits.

So everybody can use the PB method of success.

Let's now examine what is required for successful performance by studying the qualities of successful individuals. Keep in mind that the qualities outlined here are discussed in greater detail in following chapters.

THE RECIPE FOR SUCCESSFUL PERFORMANCE

Successful people improve their overall performance level by implementing a variety or all of the following suggestions:

1 SET GOALS

They set specific goals each day—competition, career and personal.

2 EACH DAY

- They arrive early, leave late and concentrate fully in all tasks—they emphasise quality and quantity of effort.
- They set the standard; they aim to be the best at everything they do.
- They challenge fellow team members—they develop a healthy competitiveness with them.

■ *Consistency is the key*

> **TIPS**
> - Set realistic and achievable goals
> - Mentally rehearse and visualise performances
> - Keep to a normal pre-event routine
> - Employ a relaxation technique
> - Develop positive attitudes

■ *Perfection comes from:*
- *Planning*
- *Preparing*
- *Persisting*

- They volunteer for difficult projects and promote 'self-confidence'.

3 MENTAL PREPARATION

They schedule periods for relaxation each day and prepare mentally to get the most out of each challenge presented. They see themselves successfully accomplishing all desired tasks. This keeps their best performances fresh in their mind.

■ *Strive to perform better today than you did yesterday*

4 LIFE-STYLE

They respect and listen to their body and accept what messages the body sends. They rest well and provide proper and adequate fuel (nutrition) for it.

5 EVALUATION

They honestly analyse and evaluate their performance by considering:
- What did they learn?
- What areas need further refinement?
- What strategies require review in order to improve?

Kieren Perkins, OAM

The 21-year-old world champion long distance swimmer Kieren Perkins radiates success in and out of the pool. Whilst busy attending to sponsorship meetings, advertising shoots, swim meets and training, charity appearances and countless media interviews, Perkins remains the ultimate role model for many Australians. Despite his celebrity status, he appears remarkably unaffected by the adulation and accolades. Diplomatic, confident and intelligent, Kieren doesn't allow his success to go to his head.

Fiercely competitive in the water, Perkins is no stranger to hard work. He commits himself daily to 'a world of pain' in which he rises at 5.15 a.m. then swims up to 15 km in the pool. The International Management Group seek to reward Perkins for his determination and talent by securing him various high-profile sponsorships and speaking engagements.

Insight into the remarkable determination and success of Perkins may be found when realising that at age 9 he badly injured his left leg when he ran through a glass door. His left calf required more than eighty stitches leaving him almost unable to walk. His desire to fully rehabilitate the injury, maximise his skills and the expert coaching of John Carew have resulted in him being unashamedly the highest profile sportsman in the country and the 'Golden Boy' of swimming.

Photo Courtesy of Tony Feder/Sporting Pix

6 SELF-BELIEF

They develop and maintain an honest and realistic self-belief. They review past achievements as reminders of why they have reached their current levels.

7 RECTIFY

After mistakes, they push themselves to rectify errors and make up for mistakes. They see disappointments as hiccups rather than a pattern that will occur again.

8 RESPECT OTHERS

They radiate confidence in others by encouraging and praising their achievements.

9 VACATION

They utilise holidays and rest to evaluate and correct work performances. They pursue activities that are interesting, challenging and very enjoyable.

10 SELF-DISCIPLINE

They discipline themselves not to retaliate or argue with others. They concentrate solely on their goals and discuss problems or frustrations with team members or trusted professionals. They never give their critics the pleasure of witnessing anything unworthy.

11 ENJOYMENT

They remember that success is a journey and not a destination. They enjoy what they achieve short term with increased endeavour and confidently expect to experience further success in the future.

QUALITIES OF SUCCESSFUL INDIVIDUALS

Successful performances result when the following qualities are exhibited consistently.

1 DRIVE AND DESIRE

They hunger and they strive.

2 AGGRESSION

Controlled and disciplined.

■ *Be a 'possibility' thinker*

3 DETERMINATION

- Nothing is impossible.
- Nothing beats them.
- Give more when needed.
- Eradicate inconsistency.

4 RESPONSIBILITY

- Take responsibility for their own lives.
- Accept self-discipline.

- Decide on courses of action.
- Work hard—luck has nothing to do with it.
- Honest with self.

5 LEADERSHIP

- Welcome opportunities to take calculated risks.

6 SELF-CONFIDENCE

- Believe in own ability.
- Positive and honest attitude.
- Displayed in action, not words.

7 EMOTIONAL CONTROL

- Monitor and control nervous energy.
- Calm, controlled, clear.

Joyce Brown, OAM

Recently retired highly successful Australian netball coach Joyce Brown, OAM, combined the qualities of genuine care for her players and strict discipline to mould an all conquering world championship team. She stressed the importance of encouraging people to believe in themselves and demanded that her players continually train extra hard to remain number one in the world.

Brown believed sport was as much a game of the mind as the heart and argued that honesty was the only way to earn respect from others. Highly disciplined and capable of making hard, crunch decisions, Brown spent countless hours pouring over sport literature and analysing endless game tapes whilst meticulously preparing for a tournament. As with the other highly successful coaches (David Parkin, Kevin Sheedy) Brown left nothing to chance, attempting to stay ahead of the opposition and always thought of new ways to improve her team. Brown's professional attitude to coaching and people management ensured that she remained one of the most successful coaches in the history of the sport.

8 MENTAL TOUGHNESS

- Act instinctively and automatically.
- Can and will.

9 COACHABILITY

- Eager to learn more and to be the best possible.

10 TRUST

- Believe in themselves and their ability to achieve.

11 COURAGE

- Confront rather than dodge.
- Will bet on self.

12 ESTEEM

- Recognise own worth.
- Reject defeatism.
- Earn respect through actions.

As you approach **each day**, go over these points in your mind:
- **attack** each contest on its merits.
- be confident of defeating any challenge.
- **do not worry** even if you make an error, but concentrate on the next task.
- **give encouragement** and advice to others—reinforce your faith in them and their ability to perform well.
- **never** forget that mind and character contribute as much to your achievement as does skill.

■ *A characteristic of successful people is that they know what they want to achieve and how to go about achieving their targets. They allow no one or nothing to stop them from reaching their targets.*

Robyn Maher

As a youngster Robyn Maher was a multi-skilled sportswoman excelling in tennis and netball and as an adult she is a consummate winner of women's basketball. Captain of Australia for 15 years and a member of nine WNBL championship teams, Maher is an outstanding athlete. She first made the national team at age 19 and is still an enduring force in the international game with four world championships and two Olympics behind her. Without doubt the best female basketballer Australia has produced, Maher is at her best when it matters most. Exceptionally competitive and committed, Maher always gives 120 per cent to the game and has set her sights at leading the 'Opals' to Atlanta for the 1996 Olympics.

Photo Courtesy of Tony Feder/Sporting Pix

HOW OFTEN DO YOU ATTEMPT THE FOLLOWING?

The following is a check-list of areas in which consistently successful individuals rate highly. In order to raise your quality of output, you should do all these things too. It will serve as an excellent starting point if you first discover how you rate on these factors.

Instructions
1 Tick the response that most accurately reflects you.
2 In the final column place the appropriate code from the list below which will indicate the amount of work you need to do for each factor.

MUCH WORK: MW, SOME WORK: SW, A LITTLE WORK: LW, NO WORK: NW

	Rarely	Sometimes	Often	Always	Code
IDENTIFY areas of your performance that require additional attention and implement a priority plan of action to improve them.					
UNDERSTAND when and how to select and execute the correct skills efficiently and effectively.					
ELIMINATE any disruptive or destructive elements in your life-style so that you can give your total energy to succeeding.					
DEVELOP the desire to always display your best efforts. Continually place yourself in stressful competition situations where you must extract excellent outcomes.					
STICK to 'the basics' that you know work for you and will assist you to overcome factors (physical or mental) capable of limiting your development.					
DEVELOP self-confidence by forcing yourself to regularly accomplish difficult tasks that require initiative and perseverance.					
MEET regularly with people who can objectively and accurately assess your progress and evaluate your capabilities.					
CONSCIOUSLY monitor your self-talk, aiming always for positive statements and affirmations of own abilities.					
DEVELOP a positive attitude towards others. Greet people with a smile. Compliment people on their positive qualities.					
USE a variety of relaxation strategies through the day, especially in times of great pressure.					
SPEND time to discover new techniques and to review performance statistics and personalities.					
MODEL yourself on a highly successful person—note the way they approach employment and sport, present themselves in public etc.					
ATTEND addresses (speeches) and read articles by people you admire.					
PRACTISE rectifying a weakness regularly.					
KEEP to a nutritious diet and well-balanced life-style.					
ALWAYS remain enthusiastic and optimistic and expect to do well.					
DO extra work—work that is not initially asked of you—to gain the additional competitive percentage that comes from extra effort.					
PRACTISE taking leadership roles and responsibilities—volunteer to tackle the projects considered too difficult by many.					
CREATE a success file of comments, appraisals, photos, reports etc. from all your performances.					

COMMON SENSE AND SUCCESS: A FINAL WORD

Common sense is a vital ingredient of the successful individual.

- Don't attempt things publicly that you haven't practised and perfected privately.
- It is rare that you will achieve much if you take this risk. Use those skills you feel most comfortable with and keep quietly confident.
- Accept responsibility for ensuring all dimensions of your skills are covered and never hesitate to seek advice.
- Routinely work out (in writing) a career plan for yourself. List exactly what you want to gain from your life and deliberately attempt to implement a strategy to achieve your targets.
- Keep a file on the strengths and weaknesses of your opponents to assist with your competition strategies.

■ *Work hard,*
Work smart

QUEST FOR SUCCESS

Consistently high achievers attempt to implement all, or many, of the following.

HOW DO YOU RATE?

		Yes	No
i	Set specific, daily goals that you wish to accomplish.	☐	☐
ii	Take time to mentally prepare before an important occasion.	☐	☐
iii	Commit yourself to demonstrating precise skills.	☐	☐
iv	Remain free from distractions—100% focussed on task.	☐	☐
v	Visualise achieving all targets on time.	☐	☐
vi	Rest well, so to remain alert and healthy.	☐	☐
vii	Discipline self to focus on what works best for you.	☐	☐
viii	Avoid wasting energy on things beyond your control.	☐	☐
ix	Draw lessons out of every experience.	☐	☐
x	Focus on action and giving more than expected.	☐	☐
xi	Try hard to rectify errors and welcome constructive criticism.	☐	☐
xii	Plan, evaluate and correct—always thinking improvement.	☐	☐
xiii	Accept responsibility regarding errors and correct without excuses.	☐	☐
xiv	Thrive in pressure situations and deliver when needed most.	☐	☐
xv	Motivated by the thrill of self-improvement.	☐	☐
xvi	Control temper and will not retaliate unnecessarily.	☐	☐
xvii	Stay logical and clear when others are hurried.	☐	☐
xviii	Laugh frequently and are always positive.	☐	☐
ixx	Prepared to risk being innovative and adventurous.	☐	☐
xx	Willing to work in a committed manner towards identified targets.	☐	☐

Highly successful teams engage in ongoing evaluation of their performances and the contributions of individuals to team outcomes. Such teams decide on how and when they will review their progress and collaboratively decide on alternative strategies to enhance productivity. Responsibility for completion of agreed targets is clearly articulated and all team members acknowledge that they are dependent upon each other for success. Interdependency encourages ownership and commitment. Consistently successful teams openly share information, provide honest feedback, appreciate individual differences and collectively commit themselves to the pursuit of excellence.

■ *Congratulate often*

How does your team rate? Complete the following check-list.

Indicate if your team is competent (strong, average, weak) in the following roles:

Characteristics	Strong	Average	Weak
Ongoing evaluation			
Sharing of information			
Honesty in feedback			
Self-directed			
Clearly articulated goals and objectives			
Respectful of individual differences			
Collective ambitions			
Encouraging of innovative ideas			
Exceptionally skilled			
Enthusiastic and challenging			

*Given the above assessment of your team, what must be done to improve its effectiveness and potential for success?

_____

_____

_____

_____

DON'T FORGET

1 Often the difference between a successful individual and a failure is not one's better abilities or ideas, but the courage that one has to bet on their ideas, to take a calculated risk, and to act.
2 Successful individuals:
   • set realistic, achievable goals and targets.
   • mentally rehearse and visualise themselves being successful.
   • employ a suitable relaxation technique when feeling stressed.
   • believe totally in themselves.
   • have a positive and encouraging attitude.
3 Successful individuals know what they want and how to go about achieving their target. They are singleminded in their determination to accomplish their goals and continually develop their skills to ensure they are better than their opposition.
4 Successful individuals aim for and will make continual sacrifices in order to obtain their personal best.
5 Successful individuals work hard, prepare thoroughly and exhibit an honest attitude.
6 Successful individuals are proud people.
7 Successful individuals have ambition and drive, and the desire and determination to succeed.
8 Consistently high achievers never quit.

■ *Minimise the gap between what you say and what you do*

WHAT ARE THE ESSENTIAL QUALITIES PERFORMERS IN YOUR SPORT MUST POSSESS TO ENSURE SUCCESSFUL PERFORMANCE?

NAME	SPORT	RESPONSE
Lindsay Gaze	Basketball	Self motivated and disciplined. Enthusiastic trainers and self-desire to be the best.
David Parkin	Australian Rules Football	High level of commitment and mental toughness. Technical expertise and physical prowess.
Joyce Brown	Netball	Self-motivation, anticipation, concentration on relevant tasks, willingness to be coached, high self-esteem, calmness.

2 HANDLING FAILURE

If we learn from disappointment and losing, we become winners in the er

Successful individuals regularly turn in performances that are PBs. They do this by working and practising hard at the factors mentioned in Chapter 1, 'Success'. But there is something else that is common to the great individuals and that will be examined in this chapter—failure and their reaction to it. How individuals react to failure determines whether or not they will go on to greater heights.

There are two sure things about the road to successful results:

1 **There will be setbacks along the way.** There will certainly be disappointments and poor results along the road to success. No high achiever has ever just simply produced one PB after another for their entire career.

2 **Failures are only hiccups, not setbacks**. The reaction to failure determines whether it becomes permanent and allows no further PBs or improved results to follow, or simply a stepping stone to success. Failure and setbacks are merely stumbling blocks. If they are learned from, further PBs are assured.

■ *Big problems disguise big opportunities*

The world is filled with many individuals of equal physical ability and talents, all of whom are capable of completing tasks that lead to success. The major reason so few achieve the pinnacle they aspire to is they fail to really believe that, even after repeated setbacks, they can still accomplish great things.

Persevere, work hard and become determined never to give up until you have achieved your goals and utilised your talents fully. Some of the most remarkable victories have taken place by people rejected, discarded or told they were not good enough and never will be.

The human mind thrives on challenges, creative and innovative plans and goals, and dulls when it is asked only to perform limiting, unimaginative and routine tasks. So don't put off tasks or skills that have proven to be too difficult to master.

Set about rectifying the situation with a realistic, intelligent and logical plan of action. Your brain has enormous capacity for solving the most troublesome problems. With adequate planning most situations can be overcome.

To fail is hard and hurts, yet eventual success often involves enormous sacrifices, pain and heartache. But to be mediocre and accepting, and never dream about climbing and conquering huge obstacles, involves the greatest pain of all.

So dare to be different, remain proud and believe that even though defeated it is momentary. Believe you can and will return to claim the prize that is rightfully yours.

THE FAILURE MENTALITY

Individuals who commonly experience failure do so because they do not accept the truth about themselves and their abilities. Instead of viewing difficulties as opportunities for growth, they impose barriers and fears regarding their ability to conquer obstacles and usually restrict themselves to a comfort zone based around inaction.

LET FAILURE EDUCATE YOU

Many individuals forget that to rectify disappointments and poor results they should reflect upon why they have failed and utilise the lessons such failures have taught them. Always remember that for successful individuals:

Failure is used as an essential experience for climbing towards success. The difficulties encountered are treated as opportunities to learn and to conquer. They are treated as they should be—stepping stones to greater, worthwhile, and often exhilarating experiences.

Unless you are willing to risk the possibility of failing or backing yourself (often against the odds) you may never really develop your skills to a level that will provide you with the possibility of consistent success. Of course, failure is always disappointing and often crushes or saps enthusiasm and courage. However, not to try again and again, to persevere and overcome obstacles in competition and life is to be eternally doomed anyway!

> **Australian Cricket Team**
> The victory by the Australian cricketers in the Carribean in 1995 was achieved despite losing their two strike bowlers (Craig McDermott and Damien Fleming) before a test ball had been bowled and without the assistance of coach Bob Simpson due to illness at a crucial time on the tour. Despite these hurdles and being considered the 'underdog' in the series, the Australians refused to be intimidated by the West Indians and claimed the Frank Worrell Trophy with a 2–1 victory.

WHY PEOPLE FAIL

In the following table, twenty factors common to people who fail have been listed. You can learn from these. Examine each carefully, and then decide honestly where you think you stand at the moment.

If you have been having problems in these areas, such assessment is the springboard for determining what action you should take to turn setbacks into stepping stones towards continued success.

THE REASONS WHY MOST PEOPLE FAIL TO ACHIEVE WHAT THEY WANT IN LIFE

INSTRUCTIONS

In the space provided after each comment, place the appropriate code from the list below that will tell you how much work needs to be done for any particular factor.

A: NEEDS MUCH WORK   B: NEEDS SOME WORK   C: NEEDS A LITTLE WORK   D: NEEDS NO WORK

		Code
1	They lack strong purpose or direction.	
2	They don't aim to be better than average.	
3	They can't be bothered to rectify and improve areas that are deficient.	
4	They lack self-discipline and don't control their negative thoughts or bad habits.	
5	They procrastinate with much talk and little action.	
6	They lack persistence. When the going gets tough, they give up.	
7	They have a negative attitude, which stops them from seeing the potential or positive possibilities in any situation.	
8	They are always looking for 'something for nothing' instead of concentrating on working hard for what they want.	
9	They don't commit themselves by making definite decisions and sticking to them.	
10	They fear criticism and honest assessment of performance.	
11	They are never willing to take calculated risks.	
12	They work with people who neither inspire nor motivate them to achieve all they can.	
13	They close their minds and lack the flexibility to entertain new ideas.	
14	They stay in situations they don't like because they perceive themselves as being helpless or unable to alter the situation.	
15	They generalise instead of concentrating all their efforts on one specific aim.	
16	They lack enthusiasm. They don't show others that they're particularly interested in anything.	
17	They fail to listen to others' views because they are reluctant to entertain the truth.	
18	They guess instead of thinking logically or getting the facts. They fail to plan and set realistic targets and goals.	
19	They refuse to ask for assistance from trustworthy professionals.	
20	They forget to show other people their enthusiasm by encouraging and supporting their ventures.	

Thomas Edison

The story of brilliant inventor Thomas Edison highlights how determination and self-belief help to overcome any obstacles. Edison was partially deaf as a boy and considered by his teacher too dull to learn. It was thought that rather than holding back the whole class, Edison would be best withdrawn from the school. In fact, it was Edison's mother who took it upon herself to teach him.

When Thomas Edison died many years later, every home in the USA turned off its lights for one minute at exactly 9.59 p.m. as a tribute to the man who had invented those lights.

Edison invented the record player, the movie projector and the electric light. The boy who was considered 'too dull to learn' had shown the world the value of perseverance and preparedness to ignore the negativity of others. Rather than accepting the opinions of those around him, Edison, with the assistance of his mother, proved that anything is possible—if you **try!**

HINTS FOR PROCRASTINATORS

1 Allow more time than you think to reach your goals. For example, if you think that completing a specific project will take two hours, give yourself three of even four hours to do it.
2 Set realistic goals, but don't set them in stone. Stay flexible.
3 Break down big and intimidating projects into smaller, more manageable ones.
4 Reward yourself after each accomplishment, large or small.
5 Make a conscious effort to realise that you cannot always be perfect. Getting a grasp on this fact helps deflate the fear of failure.
6 Begin your day with your most difficult task, or the one you enjoy least. The rest of the tasks will seem easy by comparison.
7 Keep a diary of your progress—the projects you complete each day. Read it over from time to time and feel proud of what you've done.
8 Remove distractions from your work place. Keep temptations out of your way.

Wayne Harris

The 1994 Melbourne Cup winning jockey Wayne Harris has overcome several major setbacks in his career. In November 1993 Harris was in hospital fighting for his life as an infection riddled his body. He had four operations and his heart stopped once. Twice, doctors had to amputate part of his left index finger that had become infected after it was caught in a girth knuckle. Surgeons considered amputating his hand if the infection was not stopped.

Ten years ago, he was operated on for a brain tumour and was told he would never ride again. He vowed to prove them all wrong as he does whenever anybody says something can't be done. This doggedness comes from his father, who fought three bouts of cancer before succumbing.

In eighteen years in the saddle, Harris has not been entirely lucky. He has had ribs broken, smashed bones in both feet, suffered broken hands, wrists, hip, tailbone, vertebrae, sternum, nose, shoulder and collarbone. He knows quite a bit about stitches and is deaf in his left ear.

Harris has countered every injury with a singleminded determination to never give up. His Melbourne Cup win was the finest in his extensive career and marked the return from a personal hell. His story provides inspiration to us all!

TIPS

• Don't put off tasks that have proven difficult to complete. Instead, set about rectifying the situation with a logical plan of action. Your brain has enormous capacity for solving difficult problems. Most difficult situations can be overcome.
• Those who procrastinate tend to be 'if' people. 'Ifing' keeps people paralysed and feeds uncertainty. The biggest enemy to the 'if' people are the **action** people. Rather than umming and arring—**do it**.
• One of the things that enables people to survive hardship, disappointments and failure is the ability to laugh. No matter how difficult the situation may appear, somehow you must learn to laugh at yourself and share what you have learnt from the experience with good friends.

ASSISTING INDIVIDUALS WITH FAILURE MENTALITIES

A leader can assist an individual with a failure mentality by doing the following.

■ *Failure is fertiliser for success*

1 Make the individual aware of what is being done incorrectly and demonstrating clearly the correct procedure necessary to rectify the situation. Structure a series of specific training times where the individual, under appropriate guidance, can attempt to master the skills in a non-threatening atmosphere.

2 Always provide individual encouragement and realistic (yet honest) support and feedback. They must know that you have faith in them and you will assist them to overcome any deficiency if they are prepared to commit themselves to a retraining program.

3 Set short-term and achievable goals and offer immediate positive reinforcement for every project accomplished. Emphasise **action**.

4 Educate such individuals to think and act for themselves by teaching self-regulation of thought and behaviour patterns. They are responsible for deciding appropriate action when completing tasks.

5 Highlight that all behaviour usually follows a definite predictable pattern that can be broken provided they are willing to be honest and persistent. By exercising constructive thoughts and behaviours, they can resist the impulse to be negative and pessimistic.

Alwyn Barrett

'My many years of coaching successful swimmers has taught me that if you want to be the best in your sport, total commitment, loyalty and perseverance are required. I have seen many talented individuals fail to capitalise on their abilities because of their incapacity to work hard when required and overcome minor disappointments or setbacks.

The swimmers I find most likely to perform well in pressure situations are those who are both mentally tough and very clear (focussed) in the direction they are heading. They monitor their progress daily (via goals) and always encourage their training partners and squad members to greater heights. What I find most impressive about such individuals is their willingness to dedicate themselves to training harder and remaining open-minded to new ideas whenever recovering from failure.'

WHAT SUCCESSFUL PEOPLE DO

Champions possess the ability to persevere and push on when everything seems against them. They fight on no matter what the situation. High achievers learn from their mistakes and rather than seeing situations as occasions for failure, they welcome the opportunity to review, reflect and display enthusiasm and optimism for the future—often against great odds.

Successful people refuse to be negative and train themselves to control factors likely to cause hardships. They know that through self-sacrifice, dedication and industry, great victories can be accomplished. Being free of self-imposed restrictions, they remain clear-headed and focussed at all times.

Consistently high-achieving individuals really come into their own when the going gets tough. Their controlled, positive mental approach and absence of self-questioning enables them to use all failures and disappointments as opportunities for growth and as stepping stones to further success.

■ *Courage and enthusiasm are often the difference between a successful person and a failure!*

NEVER QUIT!

When things go wrong as they sometimes will
When the road you are trudging seems all uphill
When the funds are low and the debts are high
and you want to smile but you have to sigh

When care is pressing you down a bit
rest if you must but don't you quit
Success is fortune turned inside out
the silver tints of the clouds of doubt

And you can never tell how close you are
it may be near when it seems afar
So stick to the fight when you are hardest hit
it's when things go wrong you must never quit!

DON'T FORGET

1 Within every hardship lies a gift and the challenge for change.
2 The greatest single reason for failure is lack of faith in oneself.
3 People who commonly fail are bound by inaction, indecision and fear.
4 Individuals who believe they will fail usually suffer from an inner belief that they are unworthy or not deserving of anything other than mediocre achievements.
5 People who fail often are passive rather than active participants in their life.

■ *Cultivate the capacity to turn problems into lessons and lessons into wisdom*

6 Feeling helpless, such individuals surrender their responsibility and desire for success. Their determination is easily sapped and challenging projects are perceived as too difficult to master.

7 Individuals who regularly experience failures, give in and surrender rather than risk working hard to achieve their dreams.

8 If we learn from losing, we become winners in the end.

9 Failure is usually the result of inner or mental conflict not the inability to handle an awkward situation.

10 To err is human—we are all human!

11 Failures give us the chance to discover our true capacity.

David Graham

One of the most experienced and talented basketballers in the country, Graham has played in excess of 250 games in the NBL and represented Australia on numerous occasions between 1987 and 1990.

Success tip

'Whenever dealing with set-backs, I concentrate on what requires improvement. I have a strong belief in myself and my capabilities and see it as a challenge to be overcome. I set specific, short-term goals and strive to ensure I enter each contest being thoroughly prepared.'

Photo Courtesy of Tony Feder/Sporting Pix

Photo Courtesy of Tony Feder/Sporting Pix

Jason Dunstall

AFL champion Jason Dunstall is a coach's dream. Regarded as the best full forward ever seen and exceptionally disciplined, Dunstall has averaged nearly five goals in each of his 200 odd games. His record of four premierships, four club best and fairests, three Coleman medals as the league's leading goalkicker and three top-three finishes in the Brownlow Medal is testimony to his immense talent and dedication to training.

His countless weights sessions, nights spent in goalkicking practice and the capacity to play matches whilst injured are reasons why he is held in high regard. Dunstall's other major quality is his ability to keep his cool under pressure and the capacity to display a great competitive composure—never looking flustered.

He is meticulous to the point of near obsession in making sure that whatever can be controlled is controlled and he chooses never to involve himself in on-field fights or scuffles but rather affords total attention towards getting the ball, beating his opponent and kicking a goal for Hawthorn.

Success tip

'Never stop learning, listening and looking for ways to improve your skills.'

IN YOUR EXPERIENCE, WHAT ARE THE CENTRAL CAUSES OF A PERFORMER FAILING TO BE SUCCESSFUL?

NAME	SPORT	RESPONSE
Les Stillman	Cricket	Inability to be flexible in mind and skills. Lack of dedication to training and match conditioning.
David Parkin	Australian Rules Football	A lack of commitment in preparation. Unwilling to take risks and insufficient mental strength to cope with performance pressure.
Joyce Brown	Netball	Inconsistent commitment to keep trying, listening and learning; inability to change tactics and pattern play; poor decision makers; lack relevant concentration.
Alan Joyce	Australian Rules Football	Lack of discipline, courage and skill.

John Bertrand
In early March 1995, master sailor John Bertrand and his crew had a new challenge! Their boat, the 35 million dollar *One Australia* sank to the bottom of the Pacific Ocean. Rather than being distraught at the reality of looking for an adequate replacement boat, the positive Bertrand stated how important it was that none of the crew surrender their dream of winning the America's Cup back. Even though their attempt to win back the cup failed, Bertrand's singleminded drive to never give up in the face of adversity provides motivation to all!

CHAPTER 3

CHOICE: SELF-RESPONSIBILITY

Self-regulation, self-talk and peak performance

Your future is in your own hands. You have the power to make all the decisions and choices necessary to reach your goals. It really is up to you and you alone. Self-regulation is your responsibility. Self-talk has an important role to play in developing a positive frame of mind that will enable you to accept this responsibility with total commitment. You can transform your thoughts and behaviour and push forward to higher levels of achievement.

THE POWER OF CHOICE

SUCCESSFUL PEOPLE TAKE RESPONSIBILITY FOR THEIR OWN ACTIONS

Throughout this book, various references have been made to the need for each individual to accept and exercise a choice—to take responsibility and accept the consequences of making a specific decision. It is usual that individuals who are successful have little difficulty in choosing correct alternatives and committing themselves to their fulfilment. After appropriate consideration of available options, they are prepared to make a clear and deliberate choice and consciously direct their talents towards reaching a goal/target.

UNSUCCESSFUL PEOPLE DO NOT ACCEPT THIS RESPONSIBILITY

Alternatively, the majority of unsuccessful individuals experience enormous difficulty in logically evaluating options and often believe they have little alternative or opportunity to alter their level of performance. Such people are dominated by the opinions of others and their own inability to trust themselves. They lack the courage to **stand alone** and often explain success in terms of luck or chance and ignore the fact that success invariably results from choice, the decisions made, and the plans of action that support these decisions.

■ *Seek opportunity rather than security*

YOUR FUTURE IS IN YOUR OWN HANDS

One of the greatest problems an individual experiences regarding 'choice' is the need to exercise self-discipline if one is to reach a specific goal. The statement, 'if it is to be—it is up to me', emphasises that the future is in the individual's own hands! Often victories are claimed and upsets occur as a result of a person deliberately choosing to ignore the opinions of less-informed others and to persevere until they have achieved exactly what they want. They do not compromise. They display the initiative and courage to demonstrate via **action** what is their choice.

Sir Edward 'Weary' Dunlop
The life and work of Sir Edward Dunlop, who maintained the health and morale of Australian and British prisoners of war in appalling conditions, clearly reflects the power of displaying positive attitudes and constructive choices in the face of horrendous, soul-destroying circumstances.

Sir Edward became famous as the surgeon and officer in charge of camps of POWs who laboured to build a railway under slave-labour conditions in Thailand during the Second World War. Always calm in a crisis, unwavering in his concern for others and highly disciplined and loyal, Sir Edward took it upon himself to provide leadership and encouragement to others. The example he set for all fellow prisoners reduced the mental strain of the war and maintained morale in the camps.

WHO DETERMINES YOUR DESTINY?

■ *You make you*

■ *Remember— either you control your thoughts or allow external factors to control you*

When individuals fail to exercise their right to choose behaviours and thoughts that are productive, they feel unable to control their lives; when they experience disappointments, many feel 'crushed' and become depressed. They feel victimised and adopt a self-defeating attitude of 'there is nothing I can do'. This is nonsense!

Each person has the power (via choice) to select an appropriate attitude towards their career and goals, upcoming events etc. It is essential that individuals continually exercise their choice of constructive action to rectify and improve. Choose to concentrate on the **positive**, **optimistic and enjoyable** aspects of your life and adopt an aggressive attitude towards any negative, damning and critical factors.

The Australian Netball Team
The consistent success of the World Champion Australian Netball Team is reflective of very disciplined choices. Since 1990, the team has dominated world netball and stretched their winning streak to in excess of thirty international games without loss. Individually, the players choose to subject themselves to the toughest training regimes and collectively they possess superb fitness levels.

Their secret to success has been the adoption of a clear match strategy, a commitment to ongoing excellence and an obsession with improving every facet of their game. Careful pre-planning for tournaments and individual and collective self-discipline to adhere to team rules has projected this national team into the category of 'the best ever'. Put simply, these individuals 'choose to win'.

CHOOSING POSITIVE OPTIONS

To assist you in learning to choose positive options, practise the following examples of self-talk regularly.

• **I will not be a victim to my past disappointments or setbacks.**

- I will determine the quality of my life.
- I will control my thoughts.
- I am capable of turning any situation around.
- I will not allow others to ruin my career.
- I am no longer willing to be controlled by another's negativity.

TRANSFORM YOUR THOUGHTS AND BEHAVIOUR

The following practical steps will assist you when you are feeling helpless and unable to improve your achievement level.

1 BE HONEST WITH YOURSELF ABOUT WHAT'S GOING ON INSIDE YOU

It is easier to choose new attitudes and adopt new strategies if you are clear about how you already feel—admit your disappointments and anger at not achieving your goals.

Look at what people and situations trigger your frustration or pain.

2 ACCEPT THE CIRCUMSTANCES AS FACT

Don't make excuses or approve of them—or they will occur again. Learn from the error or disappointment; look at what it taught you and put into action a plan to minimise the likelihood of these situations occurring again. This is a concrete way of exercising choice and directing your thinking and behaviour rather than allowing past regrets still to haunt you. Block out the bad and look towards the improvements ahead.

■ *Depending on how we respond, life will either lift us up or grind us down*

3 LOOK FOR YOUR BOTTOM-LINE FEELING

Remember how you felt when you failed to exercise your rights or choices—the pain, the humiliation, the loss of self-worth. Try to recall through your bottom-line feeling if there was a feeling underneath all this pain that you wanted to fight the wrongs, answer the critics, and recapture or regain the pride that is rightfully yours? Did you feel you could do better?

4 CHOOSE TO RECALL AND FOCUS ON YOUR POSITIVES AS OFTEN AS YOU CAN AND FOR AS LONG AS YOUR CAN

Remind yourself that you have talents, abilities and skills. Surround yourself with a supportive group of people and activities. This will enable you to gain confidence in your ability to achieve but also in your capacity to accept the challenge involved in every competitive circumstance.

The results of implementing these suggestions will be a transformation of thoughts and behaviour patterns. Break free from the feelings of powerlessness into the sphere of power; daily develop your choice and capacity for change. By exercising appropriate choice, you will boost your confidence and achievement levels. This of course is an essential ingredient of high achievers.

TRY IT—IT WORKS!

A major reason why individuals fail to develop their potential is because they make excuses and focus on limitations, past errors and areas of weakness rather than their capacity and possibilities for improvement. Simply, a choice needs to be made:

Either I go around feeling sorry for myself
OR
I practise turning my attention to the improvements I wish to make in my life and implement a plan to DO IT!

Australian cricketer David Boon was recently quoted as saying that a major contributing factor to his consistently good form over the years was his preparedness to be patient—to hang in and remain in control even when not striking the ball well.

CONTROLLING EMOTIONAL RESPONSES

■ *Awareness of your put-down statements will weaken their power*

It has been proven on many occasions in various arenas that consistently successful individuals are the ones who control what they can, and they control their emotional response to those things over which they have no direct control. By learning to control your emotional reactions to those things over which you have no control, you effectively control the situation, rather than having the situation controlling you—it's a key to being truly successful.

THE VALUE OF SELF-TALK

Choosing positive thoughts and behaviours will have a powerful influence on your level of success. This is because words and images function hand in hand in the brain and both have a powerful impact on self-images and achievement levels. The conversation you have with yourself (commonly referred to as self-talk) is crucial for moulding attitudes and beliefs. That is to say, self-statements and what you choose to concentrate on (either your strengths or weaknesses) will ensure that **you get what you expect to get**. This is often referred to as **the self-fulfilling prophesy**.

For example, if an individual is pessimistic in outlook, this preoccupation with negativity will cause a lowering of self-concept, even resignation ('I'm hopeless'), and manifest itself as a failure mentality when an opportunity presents itself. Usually a disappointing result is recorded further reinforcing the individual's pessimism. Why? Because the person's overwhelming choice is resignation and failure.

■ *Radiate positivity*

Photo Courtesy of Bob Thomas/Sporting Pix

Jay Stacy

Jay Stacy has played in excess of 150 tests for Australia and is renowned for his discipline under pressure, natural flair and confidence in his skills. He has become a very dependable member of the national team and is always focussed on his set tasks and team plays. A penalty corner specialist, Stacy is always quick to expose flaws in opposition strategies and to capitalise on opponent lapses in concentration.

Stacy has employed goal setting extensively throughout his career and claims that daily goals enabled him to regain necessary form after being dropped from the Australian team in 1989. Always re-assessing his own performance and keen to listen to the advice of his coach, Stacy continues to be motivated by learning new skills and the thrill of competing on the world arena.

Success tip
'I accept that its in my responsibility to remain disciplined under pressure and to remain "focussed" to my task for the whole match.'

OVERCOMING NEGATIVE PUT-DOWNS

Like an infection that goes untreated, negative self-talk with fester and spread throughout the person.

The first step in transforming such self-talk is to become **aware** of the put-downs you tell yourself because awareness will weaken their power. For example:
- I should have prepared better.
- I won't perform well.
- I can't do it.
- I'm afraid I'll make a mistake.

Constantly try to replace such thoughts with positive and optimistic viewpoints:
- I will perform well today in all tasks.
- I can improve my level of performance.
- I'll never give in.
- I think I can improve because...

Avoid the temptation of judging yourself harshly and give yourself a refreshing compliment. This may not be easy initially as you may have been putting yourself down for a long time, so much so that you have been unaware of it. However, with practice you can replace counter-productive statements with specific affirmations that are simply reminders of your competence.

It is often valuable to read over these encouraging self-statements to enhance your capabilities and expectancy or accomplishment and further success.

■ *Remember—the more you direct your thinking towards potential disasters, the greater the likelihood that your fears will become reality and disaster will occur*

Les Stillman

'In my sport (cricket) mental skills tend to be more important than physical skills. The top players are very disciplined and have learnt what they can and cannot do. They tend to radiate calmness and in matches often appear internally focussed, not willing to become distracted or upset with opposition tactics or remarks.

The cricketers who tend to fail to maximise their skill are those who are inflexible in their mind and skills. They lack the capacity to adjust to the demands of the game and usually are reluctant to accept individual responsibility (make excuses) for their performances. Often these individuals also fail to dedicate themselves to training and "cut corners" in their preparation for matches.'

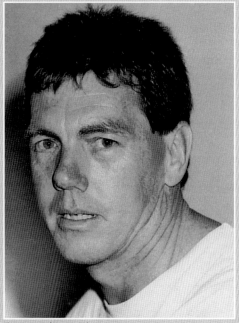

Photo Courtesy of Victorian Cricket Association

Bernard O'Reilly

The story of how Bernard O'Reilly in 1937 defied majority opinion, and employed initiative and all the courage he could muster to discover survivors of a Stinson airliner crash in the wild mountain country on the Queensland–New South Wales border, provides endless inspiration to all.

O'Reilly, an astute bushman, braved inhospitable weather conditions and terrain to find two survivors, eleven days after the plane crashed, and then organised the rescue.

Whilst most people had given up hope of ever finding the plane or any of its occupants, O'Reilly thought the plane may have crashed into the mountainous terrain due to poor visibility and low cloud. With compass and topographic map in hand and two loaves of bread, a pound of butter, half a dozen onions, tea and sugar, and a two pound jam tin, which could serve as a billy can, O'Reilly set off.

The trek was a torturous one. Visibility was limited to 10 metres due to the tangle of jungle vines and much of the 35 kilometre trip was through the unbroken, trackless ridges and gorges of the McPherson Ranges.

Despite torrential rainfall and violent winds, treacherous dense fog and low cloud, O'Reilly kept trekking towards the Lamington Plateau where, after hours of climbing and descending through soaking green jungle, he came across a mass of smashed and charred metal and the trapped remains of corpses. Below the wreck came the voices of the two survivors (Proud and Binstead)—alive after 11 days in the wilderness with no provisions. The aircraft had been tossed about in the 160 km/h winds of a cyclone and thrown instantaneously into the mountain range, 18 metres above the ground.

Although exhausted and being numb with cold, O'Reilly fed the survivors then set off to fetch a doctor and volunteers at the nearby township of Lamington. Rain-sodden and needing medical attention for numerous cuts and bruises, O'Reilly defiantly proved to others what sophisticated equipment had failed to consider—people could survive against enormous odds despite severe injury.

His story of self-inflicted hardship, back-breaking toil and courage should never be forgotten. It is an example that challenges everyone to exercise resolute determination in ensuring what begins as a dream, becomes a reality!

■ Thinking possibilities results in probabilities

WHAT LEADERS CAN DO

Leaders can assist individuals to make constructive choices by introducing the following points to them.

■ Your brain food— will it be positive or negative?

1 FOCUS ON ACTION

- This is the key ingredient of successful people—do something positive immediately!

2 QUESTION INDIVIDUALS AS TO THE INTENSITY OF THEIR DESIRE TO ACHIEVE

- What are they prepared to do and for how long to obtain their objective?
- What do they want?
- Are they clear?
- Will they accept the consequences?

3 ENCOURAGE INDIVIDUALS TO BECOME EXPERTS

- Encourage individuals to choose to learn more and develop further expertise in their specific fields.

4 TALK ABOUT CONCENTRATION ON THE PRESENT AND SELF-CONTROLS

- Be singleminded and exercise the necessary discipline to remain focussed on targets and deadlines.

5 TALK ABOUT SHARING

- Share your plans with supportive friends and performers—create a spirit of positive expectancy and mutual co-operation.

6 ENCOURAGE RECORD KEEPING

- Regularly set aside time to record privately and acknowledge personal attributes and achievements. Reinforce capabilities **—be proud of who you are and of what you achieve**.

7 ENCOURAGE DECISION MAKING

- Make decisions (after gathering all relevant information) quickly and firmly. Indecision makes the maintenance of a persistent attitude an impossibility.

8 TALK ABOUT OVERCOMING FEAR

- Daily attempt to develop courage to overcome fears of failure, of criticism, of responsibility. Identify fears and choose to replace the power unpalatable or difficult tasks have over you.

9 TALK ABOUT LIFE-STYLE

- Cultivate personal health and well being. Choose activities that relax and remove stress, eat a well-balanced diet, exercise regularly and gain adequate sleep. By doing this, your mental capacity will be enhanced and improved stamina and energy levels will enable you to work effectively and at a higher level for longer periods.

> **TIP**
> Make this choice:
> *either*
> - focus on limitations, past errors and make excuses
> *or*
> - focus on your capacity and potential for improvement.
> **The responsibility is yours.**

WHAT SUCCESSFUL PEOPLE DO

Successful individuals choose to exercise their power to reach their goals. They accept responsibility and impose self-discipline in order to accomplish what they want.

High achievers choose to display a positive frame of mind and total commitment when completing set tasks. Rather than depending on others to 'get them going', they display the courage to stand alone and implement strategies that fulfil their ambitions. Their preparedness to make clear and deliberate choices and consciously direct their talents, reflects their belief that self-regulation is their responsibility.

Such individuals often consciously choose to ignore the opinions of others and will not compromise with negative influences. Successful people display the inner strength to demonstrate, via action, what is their choice!

■ *Suffer the consequences of stagnation or face the challenges of change*

TALK SENSE TO YOURSELF

High-level achievers often through deliberate training remove self-doubts and choose to affirm and confirm the belief they have in their abilities. By removing all negativity from their minds, such achievers are structuring or programming their mind towards expecting a positive and rewarding result. **So talk sense to yourself**.

The following exercises are typical examples of how you can train yourself to concentrate on your talents and capabilities rather than past failures.

1 Complete each of the following open-ended statements:

Everyday I am getting better at _____

I like myself because _____

I am proud of my achievements because _____

I know I can _____

I am courageous when _____

I am strong _____

I am purposeful _____

I know I can improve because _____

I am a successful individual _____

One of my greatest accomplishments was _____

I can cope with pressure very well as I _____

2 State the following messages repeatedly whilst looking into a mirror:

TODAY IS GOING TO BE MY DAY, I WILL ALLOW NO ONE OR NOTHING TO STOP ME.

Activities like these are invaluable as they force you to focus attention on your strengths, talents and possible achievements. This is of the utmost importance because your brain will try to carry out the images and thoughts you give to it.

Realise that your greatest power in life is your power to choose. Being responsible and accountable will build a high self-esteem and free you from negative, restrictive programming of your subconscious.

Utilise your free choice and recognise that you deserve to be happy, free and to succeed in everything you undertake. Accept the consequences of your decisions and enjoy the profits this will bring.

Choose growth, pursue success and treat yourself and others with dignity. Doing so will allow you to achieve not only your goals but also reinforce that you are the final authority over you.

DON'T FORGET

■ *Expect the best*

1 To be successful you must accept that you determine your own destiny by taking responsibility for your own actions.

2 When you fail to exercise appropriate choices, you feel helpless and often are bound by indecision and tend to perform poorly.

3 Choose to be a person of action, to be optimistic and think in terms of possibilities. This will boost both your confidence and achievement levels.

4 **Can** or **can'ts**—what will it be? Make your brain food positive!

5 The most common weakness of most individuals is the habit of leaving their minds open to the negative influence of others.

6 What you choose to concentrate on (either your strengths or weaknesses) will ensure that you get what you expect to get.

7 Talk sense to yourself—rather than being critical, be complimentary.

8 Why sabotage yourself? Remember self-talk creates images that are reflected in achievement level. So, deliberately monitor your language—be optimistic and positive!

9 Will you give up or keep trying? It's as simple as that—**it's your choice**.

10 Successful individuals understand the inseparable relationship between the mind and the body—that the body expresses what the mind is concerned with. They take control of their lives and know:

  i **WHAT** they want

  ii **WHEN** they want it by

  iii **HOW** they can accomplish their goals

  iv **THE PRICE** they are prepared to pay for their success.

WHAT DO YOU DO WHEN YOU BECOME NEGATIVE AND BEGIN TO DOUBT YOUR ABILITIES?

NAME	SPORT	RESPONSE
Gary Neiwand	Cycling	I see myself as a battler, one who has everything to prove, the underdog which is hungry to win. This attitude makes me work harder to overcome any doubts I may experience.
Michelle Fielke	Netball	I deliberately reject any negative thoughts and concentrate on my goals. I always try to think positive, concentrate on my strengths and reflect on my previous successful performances.
Paul Wade	Soccer	I return to basics and concentrate on what I do well—I don't try anything too ambitious.
Shelley Gorman	Basketball	I make extra effort to do the small things (basics), i.e. make a good pass, block out, play hard and defensive—which helps me regain confidence.

4 SELF-IMAGE

You get what you expect to get

*The effect of self-image, your own opinion of yourself as a person, is direct and significant. How you **see** yourself is **mirrored** in your achievement levels. What you **think** about yourself is what you **become**. If you believe yourself to be second class, mediocre, ordinary or average, this will be reflected by your achievements.*

*However, **such restrictive self-opinions are rarely true**, and have usually been formed because of the put downs during your early life or because it is easier to be ordinary, to remain in the 'comfort zone'.*

*Such beliefs are not usually accurate because there is in each one of you **a potential to be much better than what you believe**. Underestimation of real potential and abilities is common. You therefore go through life deceiving yourself. The penalty is poorer achievement levels than those of which you are truly capable. A succession of personal bests will never occur under such conditions.*

Building a positive and accurate self-image** is therefore essential for every individual wishing to be successful. There is much that you can do to eliminate false and restrictive self-images. Instead, building healthy and positive attitudes opens up the doors to greatly improved performance. **All people are ordinary people; the extraordinary people are those who know it.

SELF-IMAGE IS MIRRORED IN ACHIEVEMENT

Your self-image is the foundation upon which you can build for success (or failure). If you establish an accurate, positive self-image, the goals and expectations you desire for yourself can be realised.

■ *Most limitations on performance are self-imposed!*

The manner in which self-image affects actual performance and output levels (which you can learn about in Chapter 8 'Visualisation and Imagery') is now well documented. Your thoughts and images do actually produce responses in your central nervous system, which in turn impact upon your performance.

Your mind will act on the image you give it. If you think in a way that is pessimistic and limiting, improvement in your performance and development of your potential will not occur. Your body will respond physically to the images that your mind is given. What you think and imagine is what you get.

Australia's Kieren Perkins's effort in the 1500 metres freestyle to win the gold medal and take almost five seconds off his own world record in 1991 reflected his enormous physical talent and his unwavering self-belief. A fortnight before the Pan Pacific

Games in Edmonton that year, he declared himself a certainty to break the world record. His use of self-statements were focussed on one thing only—deliberate affirmation of his own abilities and fulfilling a personal dream.

Simone McKinnis, OAM

Now a permanent member of the national netball team, McKinnis has as her trademarks mercurial interceptions, superb fitness and extreme competitiveness. Her skills and bodywork are amazing and the specialist wing defence rarely puts in a bad performance. To see McKinnis in full flight on court is to witness her uncanny anticipation and immaculate body control, which allows her to pluck an intercept without contacting. McKinnis is now regarded as the world's best wing defence and she believes her best netball still lies ahead.

Success tip

'I have always had a very strong inner resolve to play at the highest level. Throughout my career whenever I've encountered a setback I have deliberately implemented a plan to improve every facet of my game. I try to concentrate only on those variables within my control and commit myself totally to regaining form.'

Photo Courtesy of Tony Feder/Netball Australia

SELF-IMAGE MUST BE REALISTIC

In view of the significant effect self-image has upon achievement levels, it is surprising the number of individuals who have failed to truly 'know themselves'. Whilst many **underestimate** themselves since they know not of that 'vein of gold' inside, some **overestimate** their potential and abilities. Because both situations are untrue or unrealistic, no positive benefits are forthcoming.

INFLATED UNREALISTIC OPINION

■ *Realistic and consistent self-belief is the key to success*

People with such an opinion have overestimated their potential. They create enormous problems for themselves and become easily frustrated and disillusioned when their level of achievement consistently falls short of their target.

DEFLATED UNREALISTIC OPINION

People with such an opinion are very negative and self-critical and have underestimated their potential. They do not appreciate their strengths and fail to implement goals and strategies to rectify and improve performance.

Michael Jordan

Superstar Michael Jordan has always exuded confidence in his own ability to successfully negotiate any challenge he sets himself. The man who made No. 23 for the Chicago Bulls in the NBA famous has a strong sense of inner belief, and incredible desire to fulfil his dream of being the most talented athlete of all time. Jordan's unshakeable self-confidence and talent remains an inspiration to all.

UPGRADE SELF-IMAGE, UPGRADE ACHIEVEMENT

■ *Image is often mirrored in achievement level*

Many of our limitations are simply preconceived restrictions and attitudes acquired as a result of dealings with parents, teachers, friends and others during our formative years. Often these restrictions have no objective basis, yet we accept them as true. It is often said that it's not what you've got that holds you back, it's what you think you haven't got.

So for many of you, the news is good. If you have been plagued by self-doubts based upon a limiting image of yourself that may not be correct, significant changes to your level of achievement can be obtained if you can throw off these shackles.

You can improve your self-image. Since self-image is mirrored in achievement, achievement can be upgraded.

To improve your self-image you must firstly investigate your inner self to discover what strengths you really do have and what your true capabilities really are. In other words, you will be looking for the real you, not necessarily the one that has been dumped on you.

■ *If you do your very best today, your tomorrows will look after themselves*

In addition, this self-examination will almost certainly point out any weaknesses and deficiencies you have. Honest appraisal is important.

Realisation that you have underestimated some of your strengths, or that you have strengths you didn't appreciate, and the highlighting of deficiencies upon which you can work, will certainly allow you to take the first step to upgrading your self-image.

The following activities will help you achieve this.

ACTIVITY ONE: FOCUS UPON YOU

In answering the following questions, do not become confused between what you are **really** like at the moment, and what you would like to be. Answer the questions honestly after considerable thought. The object is to assist you to discover what you actually think about yourself at this moment thus highlighting areas that are inhibiting your mental approach to performance. The questions deal with the way you feel that you currently manage yourself, your personal standards, and how you would describe yourself in a period of honest 'confession'.

Instructions

Write at least six statements that sum up how you think of yourself, e.g. 'Enjoys thrill of competition'. Start with, 'I am someone who...'.

1 _____

2 _____

3 _____

4 _____

5 _____

6 _____

7 _____

8 _____

9 _____

10 _____

(*Leaders:* This is useful when individuals are meeting for the first time or for gathering additional information for planning programs.)

ACTIVITY TWO: ACTUAL SELF AND IDEAL SELF

Instructions:
Read each item carefully and then tick any item you feel describes how you are **most** of the time. This will help you to further discover what you actually think about yourself.

1   Lazy and take things as they are. ☐
2   Strong sense of purpose and direction. ☐
3   Often can't be bothered. ☐
4   Keen to work hard to improve. ☐
5   Procrastinate: talk much but little action. ☐
6   Person of action. ☐
7   Easily put off. ☐
8   Willing to persist. ☐
9   Negative: always see problems. ☐
10 Positive: always see opportunities when problems arise. ☐
11 Like to be good but see difficulties getting there. ☐
12 Willing to work hard to get places. ☐
13 Fear criticism. ☐
14 Welcome honest assessment by others. ☐
15 Always stick in your 'comfort zone'. ☐
16 Willing to take calculated, sensible risks. ☐
17 Prefer people who take things easily. ☐
18 Like to work with achievers. ☐
19 Realise situation is not the best, but content as do not think you can change it. ☐
20 Willing to take responsibility and work for better things. ☐
21 Think about good things but lack ability to focus and achieve. ☐
22 Can concentrate hard on achieving goals. ☐
23 Rarely show others any particular interest. ☐
24 Enthusiastic about everything and show it. ☐
25 Guess without really knowing. ☐
26 Always seeking and soaking up information. ☐
27 Quick to blame everyone else but self. ☐
28 Realise that whatever happens is logical and is a lesson. ☐
29 Very self-critical and destructive of self. ☐
30 Positive attitude. ☐
31 Disorganised person. ☐
32 A thinker, well organised and planner. ☐
33 Lack enthusiasm around mates. ☐
34 Cheerful and radiate confidence in others. ☐
35 Angry and impulsive under pressure. ☐
36 Calm and controlled in emotional situations. ☐

You should have learned much from Activity Two. The items with odd numbers are characteristics of poor self-image. The items with even numbers are characteristics of ideal self-image.

The work that you can do will be concerned with changing your ideas about yourself so that the 'ideal self' factors become your 'actual self'.

Now return to the activity and write the word 'me' next to the characteristics that you would like to fit you. Then complete Activity Three. In order to further examine yourself, complete the final activity using the information you have gained from the previous activities.

ACTIVITY THREE: LEARNING ABOUT MYSELF

Instructions
Answer each of the following questions on separate pieces of paper.
1 HOW DO YOU SEE YOURSELF?—What are your most vivid opinions regarding the type of person you are?
2 WHAT DO YOU LIKE?—Record the characteristics you really like about yourself.
3 SIGNIFICANT INFLUENCES?—Who or what have been the biggest influences upon you to this stage of your career? Make a separate list either for good or bad.
4 THINGS I AM GOOD AT?—List the things, whether physical or mental, and either sporting or other, that you feel you are good at.
5 UNPLEASANT OR DIFFICULT TASKS?—List the tasks or activities you find unpleasant or difficult to carry out. Write down also why you find this so and what you may be able to do about it.
6 MY EPITAPH?—How would you like to be remembered?

■ *What you think and what you concentrate on is what you become*

CHALLENGING YOUR SELF-IMAGE

Successful individuals are willing to challenge and rectify any view of themselves that is restrictive or negative. They attempt to change self-beliefs and construct a portrait of themselves as being capable, likeable and determined to make the most of all their talents and capabilities. They consciously create an impression of themselves overcoming obstacles and being successful.

This fact was proven by the remarkable success of John Bertrand and the crew of *Australia II* when they won the America's Cup in 1983. The first objective of John Bertrand was to teach everyone involved with the venture the importance of being proud, singleminded, confident and never to doubt themselves as winners. Faced with this self-belief and unerring determination, the crew won the series 4–3.

Whilst many individuals hold negative views about themselves, there is no reason why, with a legitimate desire and determination

■ *You hold a mental blueprint of yourself—reject and replace self-limiting beliefs with positive and realistic images. Success ultimately depends on how you think about yourself.*

Phil Dale

'It is my experience that strong self-belief is a hallmark of all great sportsmen. In baseball, the best players never doubt themselves and love to play in close situations—whether it be controlling the pitch and recording a strike or hitting a home run to win the series.

When pitching in a game I utilise goal setting to keep me "on track". I set myself specific tasks and concentrate on "my job" rather than the reaction of the opposition or crowd. I utilise the mental skill of visualisation extensively before each pitch and if ever feeling tense or anxious prior to competition deliberately employ slow, deep breathing techniques to calm myself down. I try to remain level-headed at all times and still enjoy the thrill and excitement of competition.'

*Phil Dale received 'Pitcher of the Year' award for his efforts throughout the 1995 baseball season.

for change, they cannot replace failure scripts for themselves with positive, creative roles that will alter their self-image and release all their talents and abilities.

GUIDELINES TO IMPROVE YOUR SELF-IMAGE

- **Self-assessment:** Make an honest evaluation of your strengths and weaknesses.
- **Self-talk:** Use affirmative and positive self-talk—radiate happiness and optimism.
- **Life-style**: Care for yourself—proper nutrition, adequate sleep and periods of rest are vital.
- **Singlemindedness**: Plan and think solely towards 'success'—be singleminded.
- **Planning**: Set attainable and appropriate goals.
- **Mental rehearsal**: Spend 5 to 10 minutes each day in a quiet place, mentally rehearsing and 'seeing yourself' achieving your goals. Focus on what you can achieve today and tomorrow rather than past actions.
- **Develop strengths**: Implement a plan—take steps daily to extend the various qualities and strengths you have. Deliberately develop your abilities.
- **Role models**: Mirror the behaviour/attitudes of other successful and respected people. Be honest in your dealings with others.

TIP

What you think you are, you really are. Therefore work assiduously on your thinking, your imagination and your visualisation in order to upgrade your image of yourself.

- **Accept challenges**: Incorporate realistic challenges into your daily program.
- **Defy self-doubts**: Refuse to give into self-doubts and 'put down' messages—accept praise when it is offered.
- **Be honest**: Be courageous enough to voice your concerns and feelings. Express honestly what you wish to attain.
- **Overcome obstacles**: When you encounter obstacles, blockages to your goals—**don't give in; intensify your desire; adopt a new, flexible and creative strategy and overcome the difficulty**.
- **Focus on achievement**: Recognise the self-discipline and sacrifices you have made to reach this point. **Be proud of who you are**.
- **Learn all you can**: Cultivate a thorough knowledge of your profession—be eager to learn more and develop your talents and expertise further.
- **Help others**: Be willing to offer advice and assistance to individuals of lesser ability—**remember where you came from**.
- **Mix with successful people**: Remove yourself from people who are negative and surround yourself with people who are keen and enthusiastic for success.
- **Seek leadership**: Deliberately place yourself in situations where you are required to make decisions and take responsibility, and follow a definite course of action.
- **Review**: Set aside a regular time to review and assess your progress.
- **Visualise**: Regularly bombard your mind with positive self-images. Remember, what you think is what you get.

WHAT SUCCESSFUL PEOPLE DO

Successful people maintain a healthy self-image and life-style by ensuring they maximise their usage of available time and resources.

The following steps highlight how to manage time effectively.

1 **Life-styles**

Establish some long-term and short-term goals and strategies that will assist achievement of each goal.

2 **Set priorities**

Goals should be prioritised: use 1 for high-priority goals; 2 for medium; and 3 for low priority.

3 **Construct a daily 'To Do' list**

Record all activities that need to be accomplished in the day and tackle the highest priority goals first.

4 **Don't procrastinate—do it now!**

Rather than hesitating and dwelling on problems, roll up your sleeves and attack the problem head on. Employ a strategy of reducing the problem into smaller more workable challenges.

5 **Set aside times for quiet, reflection and relaxation**

Escape for some precious moments to 'recharge' your energy supplies before returning to the battlefield!

Photo Courtesy of Tony Feder/Sporting Pix

Steve Waugh

Steve Waugh, Player of the Series in the 1995 West Indies cricket tour, is regarded as a great team man with a desperate desire to win. His batting average per test match against arguably the most fearsome and hostile pace attack in international cricket was over 100 runs. Waugh's double century in the final test at Sabina Park took over 9 hours to complete and was achieved despite a relentless barrage of short-pitched bowling. Battered, bruised and fatigued, Waugh displayed tons of grit and determination to ensure Australia a priceless victory by an innings and 53 runs.

The 29-year-old is amongst the world's top all-rounders and is considered by team mates as a 'real hard-nosed, very competitive bloke with nerves of steel'. Batting at No. 6, Waugh often takes the game by 'the scruff of the neck' and his tight medium-paced bowling frequently results in key wickets tumbling.

Photo Courtesy of Tony Feder/Sporting Pix

Michele Timms

'In order to be successful, you must believe totally in your ability to do any task given to you. I have found that whenever my thinking becomes negative or I start to doubt myself, I seek advice from my past coaches and top players who usually reassure me of my ability.

In games, I focus on doing the "little things well" and never dwell on mistakes too long. I concentrate on my game plan and always visualise myself stopping my opponent and winning the ball as well as shooting the ball through the hoop. I always train in a manner that reflects game situations and this enables me to perform my skills in a game automatically and without hesitation.'

DON'T FORGET

1 Self-image is the cornerstone of success.
2 Self-image is mirrored in performance.
3 The effect self-image has upon your achievement, thought patterns and general mental condition is enormous.
4 Unless you trust your own capabilities, you will always perform inconsistently.
5 Develop an honest and encouraging image of yourself. Record your abilities and frequently remind yourself of what you have achieved.
6 You often are your worst enemy and harshest critic.
7 Individuals with a realistically healthy self-image/opinion see themselves as:
   • likeable
   • valuable
   • acceptable and
   • worthy.
   Not only do they feel they are people of dignity and worth, they behave as though they are. It is this factor of how individuals see themselves that proves to be the most outstanding difference between high and low achievers.
8 What you think you ultimately become.
9 We learn who we are and ultimately live by that opinion. If you don't like what you've learned, learn something else.

The following poem highlights the importance of self-belief/image and performance.

IF YOU THINK YOU CAN

If you think you are beaten, you are,
If you think you dare not, you don't,
If you like to win, but think you can't,
It is almost certain you won't!

If you think you'll lose, you've lost,
For out in the world we find,
Success begins with a person's will—
It's all in the state of the mind.

If you think you're outclassed, you are,
You've got to think high to rise,
You've got to be sure of yourself before
You can ever win a prize.

Life's battles don't always go
To the stronger or faster one,
But sooner or later the one who wins
Is the one who thinks he can!

Anon.

5 GOALS: A MIGHTY MOTIVATOR

Goals are stepping stones to success

Purpose is the engine that drives our lives. Clearly defined, written goals are the tools that make achievement of purpose possible. Successful people can tell you where they are going, how long it will take and what they plan to do along the way. They use goal setting for mapping out and obtaining career goals or for tackling and improving skill and achievement levels. It is now becoming a common practice used by highly motivated individuals and leaders. Goals provide the stimulation and form the reason and incentive that will cause and direct your activity. They provide positive reasons for keeping going when frustrations appear and renewed hope when setbacks occur.

GOALS AND WINNING

The real meaning of winning is very plain to see if you use this powerful and influential tool. A victory against opponents as a goal has limited effect since it is available to only a few. **Instead, let it be a personal thing—a victory over yourself**. Winning means setting and achieving many personal goals, either in talents or your career, and is available to everyone. Remember also, that victory can be a bonus resulting from inwardly being a winner by becoming the very best individual that you can become.

WHY GOALS?

Constant mention has been made of the importance of being very clear in your mind in order to achieve well. To minimise the possibility of becoming distracted, many people establish for themselves personalised challenges and goals. If you fail to spend time thinking and recording (on paper) what your aims are for forthcoming weeks, the chances are you will drift aimlessly and eventually end up doing things others feel you should be doing rather than the things you feel are right for you.

> ■ *Goals enable you to bridge the gap between what you are and what you could be!*

However, successful achievers pursue their goals relentlessly, regardless of what others may think.

Establishing specific and realistic targets and priorities for yourself, which can be periodically reviewed, keeps you right on track.

It forms, in fact, a **personalised performance contract**—an agreement between you and yourself. You set out the targets and the steps. You are responsible for the action. You can fiddle with the steps any way you wish. But you are in control. Such self-responsibility is highly rewarding. By refusing to break the contract with yourself, your self-image will soar.

Photo Courtesy of Tony Feder/Sporting Pix

Stephen Moneghetti

The 32-year-old 1994 Commonwealth gold medallist trains a total of 42 hours per week and runs approximately 200 km each week. Moneghetti has developed the ability to withstand extraordinary levels of physical pain and continually sets new challenges for himself. He remains undefeated in the Tokyo Half Marathon and has recorded two world best times at the course. In 1990 he won the Berlin Marathon in the world's fastest time.

Success tip

'I utilise goal setting in everything I do—it is the key to my advancement.'

GOALS ARE STEPPING STONES TO SUCCESS

Goal setting is an extremely valuable tool for improving achievement levels. When you set a target or goal to be achieved and then set down the steps you will take to achieve the goal, **you are bridging the gap between what you are and what you want to be.** Goals are really stepping stones to success—to the achievement of PBs.

What is involved in goal setting? Can you do it? All it requires is discipline and tenacity of purpose. Carry out an evaluation, decide what you want to achieve and what you are prepared to sacrifice for it, then establish priorities and goals and **go for it**.

■ *Have big plans—accomplish them in small steps*

THE ADVANTAGES OF GOAL SETTING

Goal setting is an extremely valuable method of improving achievement levels because it provides so many benefits:
- indicates exactly what is to be **accomplished**
- clarifies **ideas**—useful for 'focussing'
- highlights the importance of **planning** specific strategies
- minimises likelihood of **drifting**—particularly when pressure is applied
- develops the concept of individual **responsibility**, ownership and accountability
- provides immediate positive **feedback**
- reinforces achievements and **rewards** initiative
- improves the **quality** of effort
- maximises **potential**
- focusses on **action**
- raises **self-confidence** levels
- assists in **recovery from injury or illness**.

TIPS FOR SETTING GOALS

Whilst creation and implementation of goals will enhance your achievement level significantly over time, there is no magic button for you to push to have this occur. It requires thought, time and hard work. What you put into it will determine what you get out of it.

Although you may start with good intentions you can become bogged down and lose the important advantages this tool has in store for you. So take note of the following very carefully.

1 PATIENCE AND PRACTICE

Simply writing down a goal and looking at it often does not work on its own. There is a lot more to it than this, but the rewards are so significant the effort and patience are well worthwhile.

2 SET CHALLENGING BUT REALISTIC GOALS

Goal statements that record that anything short of perfection is not good enough, are highly unlikely to work and are not necessary to obtain real benefits. Such statements serve only a few. Most of us lack the skills needed to be perfect.

You must think hard when setting goals. Set challenging goals but they must be what is possible.

Concentration upon setting performance rather than outcome goals, and upon several short-term rather than long-term goals as described below, can inject realism into your plans.

3 PERFORMANCE RATHER THAN OUTCOME

This is vital because whilst you can control the factors that affect your performance, you cannot control the standard of your opposition.

4 SHORT-TERM RATHER THAN LONG-TERM

Concentrate on setting several specific short-term (daily) goals rather than long-term goals. This will provide greater opportunities for immediate confidence enhancement, feedback and examples of accomplishment. Your pride and expectations levels will soar.

Also, by focussing on 'today', you are forced towards taking action **now** rather than putting things off. Do your best daily and your tomorrows will look after themselves.

5 THE INCREMENT APPROACH

Do not neglect long-term goals. They provide the direction and purpose required. Support the long-term aim by breaking it down into monthly, weekly and daily objectives to obtain the benefits of constantly reaching short-term goals.

6 FAILURE TO REACH GOALS

This will happen. It happens to everyone. It is part and parcel of the process of ultimately becoming successful. Remember, such failures are not really failures, only temporary setbacks.

Learn from them as follows:

- **Admit and acknowledge** that there will always be difficulties to be encountered. This is what striving for higher levels is all about. If it was easy, it wouldn't really be rewarding and motivating. Realising this will reduce your frustration and anxiety and prime you for increased effort.
- **Indulge in some self-examination**. Was your commitment level adequate? Were you strongly passionate and burning with desire? Was your goal realistic and achievable given your level of talent, preparation time and other priorities? Do you need to break down the goals further into smaller steps to be more realistic?

■ *Transform every stumbling block into a stepping stone*

- **Constantly reassess your situation**. From time to time other factors such as studies, illness and personal reasons may take temporary priority and require your original plans and priorities to be modified accordingly. You may need to alter your expectations and concentrate upon the essential goals only. This will be time efficient and reduce the likelihood of drastic change to your achievement level.

> **Mary Maina**
> Mary Maina, 101 years old, achieved another of her life's ambitions when she competed in the Masters Swimming Carnival in Brisbane in 1994. Maina, who has a heart pacemaker and is on daily medication, was determined to finish the 50 metre freestyle event and in doing so created a world record.
>
> Maina's swim sparked amazing scenes at the pool with spectators clapping and cheering wildly as she neared the final metres. What makes this effort all the more remarkable is the fact that Maina took up swimming at age 60 to enjoy time with her children.

HOW TO SET GOALS

1 GOAL SELECTION

Write down your goals in detail. You should write down both the long-term and short-term goals. Where do you see yourself in five years, one year, a month, a week?

Be clear and specific in writing down your goals. Write them as a direct action without any alternatives or easy outs.

Use statements such as:
- I intend to _____
- I am to _____
- I will accomplish _____
- I will handle _____
- I will be _____
- I will maintain _____
- I will master _____
- I will lift _____
- I will control _____

2 PLAN OF ACTION

Write down a plan of action to obtain each goal set.

The plan of action may involve mental practice or physical practice schedules.

Quantify everything as much as possible. Write down time-lines and target dates.

3 COMMITMENT

Commit yourself to the successful achievement of your goals with high levels of enthusiasm and dedication. Sticking it out is the hallmark of an achiever.

It is important to set short-term, even daily goals, for this purpose. Constantly achieving these little steps is highly rewarding. They make you a winner each day, and winners never quit.

4 DREAM YOUR DREAMS

■ *Dreams are cut short only by those with no 'vision'*

Your inner self takes the leading role in the obtaining of your goals. It is especially responsive to feelings and emotions. As you know, some emotions propel us to greater things and others don't.

Always, therefore, generate as much feeling for your goals as you can to help program your inner self towards successful completion of goals.

The role of visualisation in this step is vital. With all the desire and enthusiasm you can muster, see yourself accomplishing your goals and your plans of action. Practise yourself performing exactly the way you have planned.

5 CONSTANT REVIEW

Having set your goals say for twelve months, and set down all the smaller incremental steps, dates and targets, it would be most unusual if you were not required to be constantly changing these.

■ *Planning can make the impossible, possible!*

The goals can in fact become quite meaningless soon after you have set them for a variety of reasons:
• unexpected circumstances such as private commitments or illness
• you are doing better than planned and ahead of schedule
• your calculations were too ambitious and you are behind schedule.

To maintain your determination and faith, you must constantly review your situation and adjust your goals, and take whatever action is necessary.

Mark Woodforde
Australian tennis champion Mark Woodforde has had enormous international success in doubles. With his partner Todd Woodbridge, Woodforde is a three-time Wimbledon champion, a world champion and won the Australian Open Doubles in 1992. Woodforde sits down after each match and reviews his performance and constantly monitors all improvements in his tennis. His success reflects continual planning and a commitment to ongoing improvements.

---

6 REWARD YOURSELF OFTEN

Acknowledge with pride and excitement whenever you have obtained a goal and always reward yourself (e.g. dinner, clothes, day off etc.) for you have in a special way achieved a victory.

An integral and important part of this process is to **record details and display them**.

Keep written records such as diaries or note books, wall charts etc. Pin up your goals, targets, dates and plans. Record the progress you make. **Highlight** the reaching of goals. This can occur every day.

Become emotionally involved in the moment. Self-recognition and reward and the emotions that go with them provide the energy and force to go on and on.

You need these constant reminders.

MISSION STATEMENT

The importance of setting goals, and being visionary, is reflected by the fact that all major businesses and companies spend considerable time and effort devising a Mission Statement. The purpose of such a document is to articulate the vision of the organisation, define what is trying to be achieved, how they aspire to perform and the values and ethics of company. Many corporations have found enormous benefits in productivity simply from having their own people working together to achieve mutually agreed upon targets. Having a series of clear statements that reflect the vision of the organisation and where it may progress in five years from now provides guidance, definition and inspiration for all concerned. It also allows assessment of the operation—be it mediocre, successful or outstanding—to be objectively measured.

As the climate of business becomes increasingly aggressive and competitive it is the process of formulating a Mission Statement that will ensure that consistency and quality are maintained.

Alan Joyce

Alan Joyce has a remarkable coaching record within the AFL. As coach of the Hawthorn Football Club he claimed both the night and day premierships in both 1988 and 1991 and the night premiership in 1992. Joyce believes football is a basic game: 'You must win the ball and do something with it. You must fight like hell when you haven't got it and you must love your club and your team mates'. He argues that the best players are motivated from within and are totally singleminded in their desire to rise to the pinnacle of success. Joyce took the Footscray Football Club to the finals in 1994—his first year as their coach.

Success tip

'I believe that goal setting is essential in daily and weekly planning. It assists self-discipline and concentration on what needs to be achieved.'

Photo Courtesy of Tony Feder/Sporting Pix

GOAL SETTING—FOR YOUR MOST SUCCESSFUL YEAR YET

NAME:_____ **DATE:**_____

To assist individuals establish realistic and achievable goals, complete the following questionnaire.
(**Note**: Be honest when assessing your abilities as a performer.)

1 What is it you want to achieve in the forthcoming year? Be specific.

_____

_____

_____

2 What are you prepared to sacrifice to achieve your targets?

_____

_____

_____

3 What difficulties or problems are you likely to encounter in reaching your targets?

_____

_____

_____

4 What can be done to minimise the effect such problems can have upon you?

_____

_____

_____

5 What is your least acceptable level of performance?

_____

_____

_____

6 What is your most acceptable level of performance?

_____

_____

_____

7 How can others assist you in working towards your goals?

_____

_____

_____

Once completed: The leader and achiever should discuss appropriate strategies and plans to ensure the targets are met.

COMMITMENT TO YOUR GOALS

Answer the following questions, which will determine how strongly you are committed to achieving your goals.

1 What were my major goals for the past 12 months?
Personally _____
_____
_____
Professionally _____
_____
_____

2 My major achievements in the last 12 months were:
Personally _____
_____
_____
Professionally _____
_____
_____

3 In what ways do I need to improve and what strategies will I implement to do this?
Strategies _____
_____
_____

4 Who can assist me to grow as a leader?
Personally _____
_____
_____
Professionally _____
_____
_____

5 What are my greatest threats to achieving my goals?
Personally _____
_____
_____
Professionally _____
_____
_____

If you don't have a goal, make finding one your first goal!

FOR BEST RESULTS IN GOAL ACHIEVING

1 As well as setting longer term goals, which form the overall purpose and direction:
   - set **short-range** goals (day, week, month)
   - set **lower level** goals (relatively easy to accomplish)
   - set **incremental** goals (little by little, part of the big objective).
2 Get **group reinforcement** (regularly consult a support group interested in a similar achievement).
3 **Ceremonialise** the achievement (certificate, reward, dinner, trip, celebration etc.).

FOR THE LEADER

Appropriate goal setting enhances the self-confidence and motivation levels of the individual.

By establishing performance-based goals, the achiever will be able to concentrate on realistic (yet challenging) targets, which are essential for success. To be most effective, goals should contain a performance measure that can be regularly reviewed and monitored to ensure it is still relevant. If discrepancies between goals and performance persist, the leader and achiever should discuss the need for re-evaluation and modification.

The following form is useful for setting goals and action plans either by the achiever or by the leader and individual in collaboration.

DON'T FORGET

1 Goals are stepping stones to success. They provide an objective way to measure progress.
2 Goals assist the performer to clearly identify what they plan to achieve.
3 Goals, once recorded and reviewed, provide the brain with the necessary blueprint for action.
4 Mutual discussion between an individual and a leader is an effective way to establish realistic and achievable targets.
5 Goal setting encourages self-discipline, provides direction and teaches self-evaluation.
6 Effective goal setting must incorporate periodic reviews and the monitoring of progress. This provides opportunity for feedback and discussion of achievements.
7 Goals must always be performance based—think PB.
8 Goal setters usually are 'go getters'.

6 CONCENTRATION

The centre of all great achievements

Without doubt one of the most valuable mental skills any individual can possess is the ability to maintain concentration in the face of distractions when competition is at its toughest. To be sufficiently relaxed in mind and body, yet to complete the requirements of the task, is a key to ensuring high achievement levels. Without the ability to focus or centre concentration completely on essential factors, you will never realise your true potential.

Individuals who are deep in concentration often appear unmoved and unaffected by external factors and simply go about their usual routine as if it were a normal occasion. The significance of the occasion seems unable to interfere with or distract them.

Without exception, high-achieving individuals have developed an excellent capacity to control their thoughts and focus their attention on the correct factors—internal and external. Such people display composure and confidence even in the face of adversity and can focus on a specific procedure that is aimed at ensuring consistently pleasing outcomes.

DEVELOPING PB CONCENTRATION LEVELS

To improve your powers of concentration you need to be able to:

1 RECOGNISE DISTRACTIONS

Identify the factors that are likely to distract your attention or focus away from completing the immediate tasks.

2 PAY ATTENTION TO APPROPRIATE CUES

Identify the factors you must concentrate upon and cannot afford to be distracted from.

3 BLOCK OUT AND CONCENTRATE PROFITABLY

Practise and learn strategies for blocking out distractions thus enabling you to concentrate upon the vital factors you have identified.

You have the ultimate responsibility to choose an appropriate response to any distraction. Identify the responses you want to make, those that will keep your mind on the job, and practise them.

Tammy Van Wisse

The success of Tammy Van Wisse as a marathon swimmer is attributed to her extraordinary determination and courage. She is a woman who refuses to recognise that there are limits to human endurance and believes that all achievements reflect attitude and the desire of the individual to conquer their fears.

Van Wisse daily breaks through pain barriers and devotes herself to training for hours so as to establish new records in long-distance swimming. Australian swimming greats Dawn Fraser and Des Renford consider Tammy to be a remarkable world-class athlete who is totally committed to achieving at the highest level.

Success tip

'My ability to remain focussed during my swims reflects my motivation. Being in the water for 9 to 10 hours at a time forces me to confront severe pain, extreme fatigue and boredom. These battles must be conquered if I am to receive reward for all my training. So I set immediate, short-term goals (for example, swim for 5 minutes at a time) and before long I am feeling on top again. I believe that my training has taught me that my mind can conquer anything.'

WHAT FACTORS CAN DISTRACT YOUR CONCENTRATION

TIP

As your stress level rises it will be more difficult to attend to details and the likelihood of error will increase. Control your stress level and concentration levels will improve.

These are the sorts of factors that may be relevant to your situation.
- Negative remarks directed at you.
- An argument with family members or friends.
- Difficulties at work or school.
- Poor decisions by people in authority.
- Tiredness.
- Weakness and lethargy.
- Nervousness.
- Confusion and hesitation.
- Doubts about yourself and negative self-talk.
- Unclear instructions.

Photo Courtesy of Tony Feder/Sporting Pix

Emma Carney

Current world champion triathlete Emma Carney (centre in photo) constantly sets new standards and world-record times in her sport. Still considered a rookie by some, Carney attributes her success to a catchcry of 'work hard and win at all costs'. Capable of pushing herself repeatedly to extremes, the 23-year-old wants to dominate in cross-country and athletics as well as triathlons. Driven by a desire to prove her critics wrong, Carney often appears unbreakable—her unbelievable performances signifying the stamp of a world beater!

Success tip

'Whenever competing, I ensure my mind is focussed on exactly what I want to achieve and I ignore any distractions around me.'

TIPS FOR AVOIDING DISTRACTIONS

The following are useful strategies to avoid distraction thus enabling you to remain focussed on the important parts of your performance.

1 **Try to relax**—slow, deep breaths are best.
2 **Set mini goals**—daily challenges to be overcome in the face of adversity (focus on what you are capable of).
3 **Reassure yourself**—believe that you can handle any situation and perform admirably even against continual negativity and aggravation.
4 **Project a positive state of mind**—always be confident and optimistic. Do not be drawn into situations over which you have no power. Refuse to get caught up in anything other than the task at hand. (Remember, you have a job to do—to perform at your best.)
5 **Identify what you can cope with and what factors must be ignored**—walk away from detrimental factors.
6 **Remove yourself** immediately from any factors or personnel that are not positive or constructive to your overall attitude and performance.
7 If the distraction is fear (fear of performing poorly), **develop strategies to reduce the impact of self-doubts**. Be ready to apply an assertive phrase or statement to counteract the tendency to be negative.
8 **Always return to the basics and the fundamentals** when feeling distracted.
9 **Prepare thoroughly and divide the challenge into smaller or manageable segments**, which must be negotiated separately—one at a time.
10 **Think only of the next performance**—you are only as good as your next contest, so give it your best shot.

HOW THE LEADER CAN HELP

It is important that each individual be aware of exactly which specific factors require attention when completing a task. Clear, explicit guidelines and examples will assist the achiever remove any likelihood of becoming confused.

The ability to shift attention and maintain effective concentration are essential skills and are capable of being learnt and improved.

Just as individuals vary in their ability to concentrate on specific tasks, so they vary in their ability to respond appropriately to stressful situations.

Whilst personally more demanding and time consuming, providing individuals with task-specific instructions is more effective. Always follow this principle: **individualise—do not generalise.**

The most effective concentration will only take place when the individual is relaxed, not confused by too many instructions, and feeling in control of the situation. Each individual must know what is essential to concentrate on and what is to be ignored in each specific situation.

> ■ *The ability to concentrate is often the deciding factor in competition—individual or team endeavours*

> ■ *Concentration is best achieved by focussing on the task at hand—the here and now*

Kasumi Takahashi

Australia's most promising rhythmic gymnast, Kasumi Takahashi, won a total of five gold medals at the 1994 Commonwealth Games in Victoria, Canada. The 14-year-old's achievements reflect her daily commitment and concentrated effort in improving her repertoire under the watchful eye of her Russian coach, Olga Morosova. A typical day for the Los Angeles based Takahashi begins in the gym at 5.30 a.m. and then she trains until 8 a.m. School commences at 8.15 a.m. and concludes at 3.30 p.m. whereby Takahashi rests until 4 p.m. before another 2 hours of training and then sitting down to an average of 4 hours homework per night. This daily ritual highlights the quietly spoken high school student's self-discipline and determination to challenge the dominance of the European gymnasts, especially the Russians and Bulgarians.

The concept of concentrated effort is highlighted by reading the following story of a stonecutter.

The stonecutter breaks open giant rocks as a result of a multitude of concentrated efforts with his hammer. This effort of repetitive hitting may not eventuate in the slightest crack but the stonecutter knows that just because you don't see immediate results from your current actions, it doesn't mean you are not making progress.

The continued concentrated approach of many hundreds of hits at different points in the stone suddenly can cause the rock not simply to chip, but literally 'shatter'! It is not the single hit that breaks the rock open but the determined and concentrated application and discipline of the stonecutter.

Photo Courtesy of Tony Feder/Sporting Pix

Gary Pert

The Collingwood champion has played in excess of 200 AFL games. His performances reflect grit, persistence and the ability to recover from two major knee operations (both of which required total reconstructions).

Pert is a specialist full back with excellent kicking and marking skills. He is highly regarded throughout the AFL as a complete player with few weaknesses and constantly sets personal goals to assess his progress and to maintain his on-going improvement.

Success tip

'Successful people have the capacity to concentrate on their goals, remain controlled in their aggression and are relentless in their desire to be the best.'

So it can be for you—the continued concentrated efforts can 'shatter' any giant rock or obstacles that are blocking your path to success.

Bathurst Motor Racing

The Mount Panorama circuit at Bathurst is the holy grail of Australian motor racing with 40 000 fans lining the track and over 10 million viewers throughout Australia and New Zealand glued to their television watching the annual battle.

The capacities of the drivers to concentrate totally are tested to the extreme as they travel at speeds in excess of 200 km/h for each of the 161 laps (1000 kms), which takes over 6 hours to complete. Precision-planned race strategies and slick pitstops during refuelling and brakepad changes by all members of the support crew are vital in deciding the ultimate winner.

Failure to attend totally to the specific requirements of the race (either on or off the circuit) results in spectacular smashes and the possibility of serious injury occurring.

DON'T FORGET

1 Concentration demands of the individual to 'come into the now' and attend to the task at hand. Train yourself to direct all your attention on one specific task.

2 Consistent achievers know what are the appropriate cues on which to concentrate and how best to ignore distractions.

3 Optimum relaxation and concentration go hand in hand.

4 Often you cannot stop a distraction from occurring. However, you can alter your response to it.

5 As an achievers' ability to concentrate can vary according to situational and personal factors, a leader must ensure all instructions are individualised and simplified.

6 Concentration and the ability to remain clear-headed usually deteriorates as stress level rises. The higher the stress level, the poorer the attention to detail and the greater the likelihood of error.

7 Like all skills, concentration levels can be improved via regular practice at imagery and assistance from the leader.

7 CONFIDENCE

First be a believer to be an achiever

To be successful consistently, you must possess a realistic and unwavering level of confidence in yourself and your ability to execute specific skills whenever required. Confidence is acquired as a result of hard work, positive thinking and determination to achieve your best always. Without confidence, you will never be capable of achieving consistently, particularly in pressure situations, because your inner belief will be that you are not capable of initiating and maintaining high-level performance. You will usually give in or self-destruct (via negative self-talk) and achieve spasmodically.

Confident individuals are people of action. They tend to be doers, and perseverance and dedication are their hallmarks. They think in terms of 'challenges' and always display a positive expectancy. They are prepared to think more in terms of 'what can be gained', rather than 'where will I fail', and are always honest in their evaluation of their capabilities.

Let's find out how much confidence you have in yourself.

IMPROVING YOUR CONFIDENCE

Because confidence is such a vital component of consistent high-level achievement, it is important that you reward yourself for all positive attempts and achievements. This will reinforce an expectancy of continued achievement and success. Highlighting pleasing outcomes can raise your self-image and alter thought patterns substantially.

The following suggestions will assist you to improve your overall levels of confidence.

1 FOCUS ON THE POSITIVE THINGS YOU ACCOMPLISH EACH DAY

Practise repeating affirmative statements about your skills and attitudes. Perhaps write one particular phrase on a piece of card and always carry it with you, e.g. 'Today I will display initiative in all tasks and encourage all people'.

Shane Dye

Sydney jockey Shane Dye is a role model for those who believe in the power of positive thinking and how to achieve whatever you set out to do. Described as the 'ultimate professional', Dye concentrates solely on winning (he has ridden for more than $12 million in the past two years alone) and radiates confidence in all he undertakes. He is keenly competitive by nature and is always in demand for rides. Why? Because he believes in his ability to ride winners—a very attractive proposition for trainers!

Photo Courtesy of Stuart Milligan/Sporting Pix

Andrew Gaze

Australian basketball phenomenon Andrew Gaze is an outstanding player who remains remarkably unaffected by his success. Always quietly confident, Gaze gets better each year and is the National Basketball League's premier player. The prolific Melbourne Tigers guard combines heavy scoring, lashings of assists and buzzer-beating baskets to hurt every opposing team. It is Gaze's consistent excellence and confidence in his ability to execute match-winning plays that makes him indisputably number one.

Opposition coaches virtually concede 30 points to Gaze and Magic coach Brian Goorjian believes he is the Australian answer to former NBA superstar Larry Bird. Gaze has worked tirelessly to become the complete player—he can rebound, make a pass, exercise court sense and is fiercely competitive.

In 1994, Andrew Gaze surpassed the 9000 point mark to become the most prolific scorer in league history. His consistency, efficiency and leadership are truly remarkable. He is a major reason for basketball being the fastest growing sport in the nation.

2 CREATE A PERSONAL REWARD SYSTEM

Whenever you have conquered a goal or achieved an aim—reward yourself. Recognise and be proud of your accomplishment and give yourself a treat, e.g. a favourite meal or a movie. Use this experience to:

- Further illustrate your ability to achieve and overcome obstacles
- Develop an even stronger belief in your success capabilities.

3 SET SELF-GOALS/TARGETS

Setting targets, knowing exactly what you want to achieve, and being definite and specific has numerous benefits for confidence building. Keep a **Goals Diary** and record daily all occasions where you exhibit constructive action and pursue a plan of attack to achieve a goal.

> **TIP**
> Systematic goal setting is the key to developing that elusive self-confidence. Constant obtaining of daily challenging goals is highly rewarding and confidence then feeds on itself.

4 VISUALISE YOURSELF ACTING POSITIVELY AND ASSERTIVELY IN A VARIETY OF SITUATIONS

Formulate and stamp indelibly on your mind a mental picture of yourself as succeeding. Hold this picture tenaciously. Never permit it to fade. Your mind will seek to develop this picture—never think of yourself as failing. Always picture 'success' no matter how badly things seem to be going at the moment.

5 CREATE AND MAINTAIN A SUCCESS FILE

Collect articles on people you admire, record your personal triumphs and file all compliments, photos and letters of praise written by people you respect. Train yourself to pursue individual excellence and regularly review (and relive) the many positive skills and personal qualities you possess and display. Identify and relive your greatest achievements. This can be very powerful.

6 PLAN TIME EACH DAY TO REMAIN HEALTHY AND RELAX

Set aside time to exercise and care for yourself.

Maintain a healthy and nutritious diet and train yourself to become aware and more sensitive to how your:

- mind is functioning—are you clear, optimistic and happy?
- body feels—are you tired, listless, feeling tense?

7 MONITOR SELF-TALK

Refuse to allow negative people to upset you or reduce your desire to succeed—see their attitudes as challenging rather than destructive forces. Deliberately change your self-talk so that statements that restrict your confidence, such as, 'I'm nervous and I rarely achieve high results when I'm nervous', are replaced with statements that build up your self-esteem, such as, 'I'm nervous but in control—I will achieve well today'. So whenever a negative thought concerning yourself comes to mind, deliberately voice a positive thought to cancel it out.

8 CONSTRUCT A CONFIDENCE LIST

Construct a list that contains attributes that you like about yourself, and your strengths, aspirations and achievements. Regularly update this list to include recent accomplishments—times when you were really proud to be you. Use your disappointments as a means of learning and growing and then forget them.

■ *Confidence comes with preparation*

9 DEVISE YOUR OWN 'CONFIDENCE RESOURCES'

- Record affirmations on a cassette tape and play them whenever you can:
  — Nothing, absolutely nothing, will stand in my way.
  — I will achieve and be successful!
  — I can do this.
  — I am in control.
  — I believe I will do well!
- Write your affirmation on a piece of paper twenty times.
- Say positive statements out loud to yourself and make them in the first person. This will become your automatic self-talk.
- Write your positive statements on small cards and carry them with you.

Vicki Wilson

The Australian netball goal shooter Vicki Wilson is a supremely confident player. Named Australia's 1994 Netballer of the Year, Wilson is always making to expand her repertoire of skills and is regarded throughout the world as a deadly accurate shot. A true perfectionist, Wilson never skimps on practice with 200 shots per day and she prepares meticulously for every contest. Her confidence stems from knowing she has done the hard work and is in total control of her netball destiny.

The champion Queenslander boasts a conversion rate that is rarely bettered by any player in the world. Her ultimate goal is to shoot at 100 per cent accuracy in international competition and her singleminded belief in her ability may ensure this goal is achieved at the World Championships in 1995.

Vicki Wilson has represented Australia on 58 occasions in international competition and is in her tenth year as part of the Australian team.

Photo Courtesy of Tony Feder/Netball Australia

10 LOOK CONFIDENT

Walk tall, keep you head up and look people in the eye when they talk to you. Speak clearly and assertively—raising your voice will release inhibitions. **Smile, encourage and congratulate**. Deliberately inform your friends of the faith you have in them.

11 AVOID COMPARISONS

Don't get locked into comparisons with others—never try to be someone you're not.

12 CHALLENGE YOURSELF DAILY

Daily set yourself a challenge—actually do tasks which are difficult. This will affirm your strength of character. Be prepared to hurt a little—develop a thick skin and don't give in. Be prepared to act! Make a list of activities you believe you are not confident enough in and daily attempt to complete a task from the list.

Frances Murphy
Three times Victorian ironwoman champion Frances Murphy enjoys pushing herself to the limit and seeing how fast and how hard she can go. Balancing a full-time career as a sports journalist with a gruelling training schedule presents many challenges, yet Murphy knows that a champion has never made it by 'turning off the alarm and falling back to sleep'. The 23-year-old believes that you get out of life what you put into it and she says that all the hard work and sacrifices to become number one in the sport have been worth it.

Success tip
'My confidence is very closely connected with my training. When my training has been demanding, I believe I can overcome any obstacles put before me.'

CONFIDENCE-BUILDING ACTIVITY

This activity is useful in identifying your various capabilities and positive attributes.

NAME:_____**DATE:**_____

Instructions
Complete the following statements and share responses with another person.

1 Something I do well is _____

2 Something I'm better at is _____

3 I can _____

4 I am proud that I _____

5 My greatest strength is _____

6 I can help others to _____

7 I need help on _____

8 I have the power to _____

9 I was able to decide to _____

10 People can't make me _____

11 I want to be strong enough to _____

12 I'm not afraid to _____

13 Something that I can do now that I couldn't do last year is _____

14 I have difficulty dealing with _____

15 I have accomplished _____

16 If I want to, I can _____

17 Strong, independent people _____

18 My greatest achievement is _____

19 I admire _____

20 I have the courage to _____

Note: This activity highlights the multitude of talents you possess. Concentrate on developing this list further rather than spending valuable time on what you cannot do!

> **Linford Christie**
> Linford Christie is the sprint champion of the world. He holds the Olympic, Commonwealth and European 100 metre titles. Whilst an exceptionally skilled athlete, Christie's mental attitude is the most important factor in his success. He is totally singleminded, focussed on winning and prepared to push himself continually to the limit. Christie radiates confidence in himself and believes that 'at the end of the day if I'm 90 per cent and the other guys are 90 per cent, they lose. If I'm 90 per cent and they're 100 per cent, they lose. If I'm 100 per cent, they've got no chance'.

FOR THE LEADER

■ *Always encourage*

It is common that individuals who are positive and confident are usually the most successful. By utilising the various suggestions in this chapter, you can become more aware of your feelings and thoughts and implement deliberate strategies to build confidence levels. Self-awareness and self-knowledge (understanding why you do what you do) brings with it great power and by persevering with these strategies, you will discover how to rid yourself of negativity and enhance your confidence and performance levels.

■ *Everyone needs to feel of value— to be recognised for their uniqueness*

On the other hand, individuals with low levels of confidence are often overlooked unless time and effort is taken to listen and be sensitive to how they see themselves and their abilities.

Always remind yourself that what you say about others and the way you treat people will influence how they feel about themselves. If you praise and encourage others long enough and with enough conviction, eventually they will believe it to be true. This is the basis of the self-fulfilling prophecy—you get what you expect to get.

So if you want to help people to be self-confident, you must believe and have total confidence in them. Obviously, it is best if you encourage these individuals to develop a realistic sense of what they can accomplish based on their true competencies.

WHAT SUCCESSFUL PEOPLE DO

Truly consistent achievers radiate confidence. They attack obstacles without fear of failure and always expect to be successful. Such individuals reject self-defeating thoughts and deliberately train themselves to look forward optimistically to the challenges that lie ahead. They are people who inspire, people who thrive on proving others wrong, people who delight in creating confusion and dismay in their critics.

Successful individuals display a deep inner faith in their own ability and in their right to achieve great things. Their optimism and self-confidence stems from the fact that their preparation has been extraordinarily thorough. Countless hours of well-planned, hard work have been invested and many sacrifices have been endured.

Universally, confident individuals are people of action.

Dedication and perseverance are their hallmarks. They tend to be doers and display unwavering strength and unshakable faith in their abilities. Their inner confidence enables them to accept that no matter how grim a situation may seem, it can and will be overcome.

Nick Faldo

Champion English golfer Nick Faldo exudes confidence in his own ability to negotiate the most challenging of golf courses. A perfectionist by nature, Faldo claims that his reputation as one of the world's best golfers is due to a painful brew of blood, sweat and tears. In 1986, in search of an improved swing, Faldo went to David Leadbetter and then would hit up to 1500 balls a day, occasionally causing his hands to bleed, in an attempt to rectify and master the swing.

Faldo's confidence not to snap under pressure comes from his willingness to practise until he can perform the skill correctly without thinking.

No one ever drowned in sweat!

DON'T FORGET

1 To improve your confidence levels, deliberately concentrate on what you **can do**.
2 Realistic self-confidence is crucial for consistent achievement.
3 Confident individuals tend to be people of **action** and think in terms of **challenges**.
4 By acknowledging and promoting individual achievements, you can create an atmosphere of expectancy based around success.
5 Confidence and courage levels can be improved provided the individual is prepared to implement deliberate strategies—as outlined in this chapter.
6 Individuals are usually most confident when people display total faith in them.
7 Daily attempt to complete tasks that prove difficult. This builds your determination to overcome all obstacles in your path to success.

8 VISUALISATION AND IMAGERY

See it clearly, believe it totally, do it successfully

Increasing numbers of achievers are using visualisation to overcome problems or develop skills. Provided you are prepared to practise consistently, it will work for you too by triggering the success mechanisms in your mind.

■ *By systematically practising skills through visualisation, individuals can actually make their body believe they are practising the skill*

HOW VISUALISATION WORKS

The nervous system cannot tell the difference between an actual experience and one that is vividly imagined. Clearly imagined situations produce impulses in muscles similar to that produced by actual physical execution of the situation. Thus, whether you perform movements or vividly imagine performing them, similar neural pathways to the muscles are used, and the brain can tell no difference.

Therefore, if we picture ourselves performing in a certain manner, it is nearly the same as the actual performance.

For best results follow these steps:

1 You must have a clear picture of what you wish to achieve.
2 Spend time daily, in quiet and relaxed circumstances, visualising (seeing) yourself achieving your goal or target. We all have the capacity to dream, to visualise pictures, patterns and plans in our mind. Practise being calm and still—this will assist your dreaming.
3 Trust your imagination and success mechanism and wait to reap the rewards.

■ *When you visualise, you are developing a picture upon which the subconscious mind works*

Imagine what you would like to achieve, and then picture this vividly in your mind. Practised regularly, this technique can change your life.

EXAMPLES: USING VISUALISATION TO ENHANCE ACHIEVEMENT LEVELS

1 SUCCESSFUL PERFORMANCE

Constantly see yourself performing skilfully and successfully.

Photo Courtesy of Stuart Milligan/Sporting Pix

Sue Stanley

'I have learnt to redirect my pre-event nerves and self-doubts into positive energy and images. I confront my fears by ensuring that before I enter a competition my preparation has been very thorough.

I have deliberately structured career goals, which are definite and attainable, and always look to take my performance in competitive aerobics to a new level. I believe that I possess the necessary levels of determination and discipline to keep me at the top of my sport and want to remain World Champion for as long as possible.'

Success tip
'To be number one in the world you need to be very determined, disciplined and very clear about ways to improve your skill routines. I use goal setting and mental rehearsal to enable me to perform exactly the way I want.'

2 POSITIVE SELF-IMAGE

You are what you think you are. See yourself as a confident, skilful and worthwhile person handling the kinds of situations you will confront during your career.

3 GOAL SETTING

Practise the setting and obtaining of goals and targets.

4 CONCENTRATION

■ *Visualisation prevents mistakes*

See yourself handling distractions and remaining calm under pressure. Rehearse important routines and pay particular attention to the cues that you find are most important.

5 CONFIDENCE

See yourself as a person of action and accepting challenges, which you handle successfully.

6 RELAXATION

See yourself in a calm state and being able to handle problems and times of possible high anxiety. You can even control physiological responses such as a racing heart beat, and blood and skin temperature.

7 MENTAL TOUGHNESS

See yourself successfully in all types of situations that require you to exhibit all the characteristics of a mentally tough individual.

8 IMPROVE SKILL LEVEL

Practise any skill by performing it in your mind.

9 SOLVE SKILL PROBLEMS

Use imagery to critically examine all stages of a problem to uncover a fault.

10 A WINNER

See yourself as a winner.

THE RESULTS OF VISUALISATION

If you visualise and imagine yourself successful (that is, achieving at your own personal best) you will begin to behave like a successful person. If you truly want success, remember this formula:

- Think like a champion
- Act like a champion
- See yourself as a champion
- You will then behave like a champion.

It is vital that you hold on persistently to your vision (goal) with unqualified faith and use every opportunity to demonstrate the

Andrew Collins

The Hawthorn Football Club champion has played in over 170 senior games, three premierships and reached the top of his sport because of his total dedication to, and obsession with, hard work. Collins's passion to learn and improve has carried him to 14 appearances for his state and to a Best and Fairest award. His devotion to being successful in football is reflected in his fierce competitiveness and hatred of being beaten. A full-time footballer, Collins loves the challenge of competition and spends hours each week studying upcoming opponents and developing strategies to defeat them.

Success tip

'My use of visualisation is very closely related to my goal setting. Once I've set my goals, I can see myself, in match situations, beating my opponents. I like visualising myself breaking packs open and chasing players, laying a tackle and bringing them down. I find visualisation helps my confidence levels enormously.'

Photo Courtesy of Tony Feder/Sporting Pix

necessary desire to accomplish it. In doing this, your thoughts are directed towards the creation of the desired goal—this is extremely powerful.

Definite movements towards your ideal image and goal will begin automatically, so make sure to imagine only the greatest ideals and aspirations. Be realistic, but aim **high**.

The only major limitation to visualisation and imagination is the extent to which you employ it. Its potency is based on persistently holding to a desired, fully accepted and completely believed-in mental picture of success.

Visualising being successful can provide several immediate benefits to your achievement levels. First, you will find your concentration vastly improved because you have activated the success mechanism in your mind, and will not be distracted by negative or petty thoughts that have no bearing on your progress.

In addition, **having your goal in constant view, you will overcome psychological blocks** (the 'I can'ts', 'I'm afraids' and the 'I don't knows'), which would have otherwise impeded your

> ■ *Allow yourself the opportunity to dream—see yourself achieving what you want and then implement an action plan*

improvement. The point then becomes not 'will I succeed' but rather 'I know I'll succeed; I can see it clearly in my mind'.

This concept is similar to the Zen principle of seeing with the mind's eye. What you are in effect doing is projecting only the image of successful achievements and all this entails for you.

The visualisation process is highly motivating. It gives shape and form to what was previously a fleeting, abstract concept. You can now 'see' your desired objective, and move towards it.

■ *Never permit the image of yourself being successful to fade*

If you believe the goal you desire is available, if you clearly and distinctly imagine yourself in full and complete possession of this goal, and if you feed that, each and every day moves you in the direction of your objective. You are not a dreamer, you are a creator—**a creator of your destiny**.

Put your imagination to work. Mentally make your plan, goal or ideal. Give it shape, form and clarity. Then hold that picture in your mind confidently and persistently. Do not force or coerce this image, but with total confidence and powerful desire, envisage the objective with complete faith.

HINTS TO IMPROVE YOUR VISUALISATION TRAINING

1 RELAX

Research indicates that imagery is most effective when combined with some form of relaxation technique. Calm body—clear mind—correct images.

2 FROM BEHIND THE EYES

Where possible, you should see the image of yourself from an internal perspective. That is, from behind your own eyes rather than from outside your body.

3 REALISTIC TARGETS

■ *Dreams are cut short only by a lack of vision*

Set yourself realistic targets. Picture yourself achieving things that are beyond your physical limits but you honestly believe you are capable of accomplishing.

4 QUIET PLACE

Free yourself from distractions—imagery is best carried out in a quiet, comfortable setting.

5 REGULAR TIMES

Set aside time daily to systematically use imagery. Before sessions (to prepare), after meetings (rectifying errors and re-affirming pleasing aspects), and, if appropriate, throughout the day (time out, resting).

6 EVALUATE

Maintain a written record of how successful the imagery is for you. Evaluate which techniques seem to be beneficial and monitor your progress.

7 INVESTIGATE

Investigate the availability of commercially produced imagery/instructional tapes. Experiment with how you can incorporate the suggestions on the tape into your life-style.

8 REALISM

For best results, individuals should picture themselves completing specific tasks in correct attire, conquering tension and delivering skills correctly.

Photo Courtesy of Norman Bailey/Sporting Pix

Brian McNicholl

'I have been extremely fortunate to travel extensively and meet many world-class athletes. I have participated in six Paralympics and believe that the best "lifters" have the ability to handle pressure when competing and always display a look of confidence about them. They produce big results when needed and remain totally positive about their performances. They also understand the critical value of programming their mind and will repeatedly rehearse the complete lift focussing on the part of the body that is most intensely involved in the bench press.'

Success tip

'I use visualisation in all my lifts. I focus on the part of the body which is most intensely involved in the lift (arms, shoulders, chest).'

DON'T FORGET

1 See it—clearly.
   Believe it—totally.
   Do it—successfully.
2 Clearly imagined events produce impulses in muscles that are similar to those produced in the actual physical execution of the event. Therefore, by picturing yourself performing in a certain manner, it is nearly the same as the actual performance.
3 Your mental picture of yourself is the strongest force within you so why not imagine yourself being successful?
4 It is the responsibility of each individual to program his or her mind so that the body will function correctly.
5 When imaging, use all senses (i.e. sound, smell, touch, taste and sight) to recreate or imagine the desired experience.
6 The only major limitation to visualisation and imagination is the extent to which you employ it.
7 Through visualisation, you can paint your own picture of success—be the creator of your own destiny by constantly 'seeing' and 'moving towards' the desired objective.
8 Like all skills outlined in this book, visualisation works best when practised daily and you hold to your desired picture persistently.
9 Often the greatest achievements are at first dreams.
10 Mental imagery and visualisation are most valuable when you are relaxed, free from distractions and clear in your mind regarding what it is you want to achieve.

A WORD OF ADVICE

■ *Whose responsibility is it for programming your mind? And what are you going to do about it?*

Don't give up on visualisation and imaging if it seems difficult at first. It is new to your mind. You haven't used this great power, and like anything else it takes time and practice to pay off in a big way. **Practice is essential.**

So, how about it? Will you visualise yourself as a success and imagine reaping all the rewards that can be yours or will you just imagine that success only happens to others and not you? It's up to you. In your life, you can be as big or as little as you wish.

Remember: **'The me you see, is the me you will be'.**

What me will you be?

9 RELAX YOUR WAY TO PERSONAL BESTS

Whenever relaxed and calm, we are linked to our inner power

Relaxation is the key to achieving repeated success. The individuals most likely to succeed are the ones who 'hang loose' in stressful situations. They are never too tense or aroused. They have learned to use relaxation to control both excessive mental and muscular tension and never allow them to interfere with their achievement level.

Mental calmness is an increasingly precious commodity in the frantic world of the 1990s. Research continually informs us that the human mind does not function effectively when it is rushed— creative solutions commonly arrive only when a person is calm and feeling 'in control' of their life.

Becoming tense, uptight and agitated about problems only creates further difficulties. Solutions are being found when all options are calmly considered.

Calmness also keeps open lines of communication by which creative ideas will flow to you.

POOLS OF SILENCE

People who value their health, fitness and performance efficiency, create for themselves 'pools of silence' whenever they can by retreating into a place of quietude.

Silence has a creative value when used to think, reflect, recall past enjoyable experiences and to contemplate all we have to be thankful for.

In silence we may define our aims and assess our progress towards achieving them, and face problems and work out ways to solve them.

Success often rides on a rushing wind, a roar of flames and a rumble of thunder. There is much to be gained from regularly breaking, and diving into, the pondering pools of silence.

THE VALUE OF RELAXATION

Individuals who have learned how to control themselves through the use of relaxation techniques are more likely to turn in repeated best performances than those who do not have this mental skill.

Used during the day, relaxation leads to more precise skill execution and higher levels of correct decision making, particularly in times of great pressure or distraction.

Learn to handle pressure successfully by:

- relaxing
- exercising to channel off physical or mental tension
- controlling thought processes in tough situations
- confronting the challenge of tough situations positively and calmly.

WHAT IS RELAXATION?

It makes good sense to learn how to relax. In competitive situations you must be able to avoid unnecessary fatigue and improper muscle tension, and you must maintain an optimum (appropriate) level of anxiety by avoiding high levels of mental tension (causes memory loss, inability to concentrate). Both of these will have detrimental effects upon your skill performance.

David Wansbrough

Wansbrough is a veteran of 170 tests and was a member of the 1992 Australian hockey team to win a silver medal in Barcelona. A confident and determined player, Wansbrough is widely regarded as a player who can stick to a task, control his feelings, and ignore distractions such as tiredness, opponents tactics or umpiring decisions until the ultimate result is obtained.

If ever anxious prior to a major performance, Wansbrough uses music to calm himself and then applies breathing techniques to relax completely. A constant encourager on the pitch and a reliable performer in big matches, Wansbrough continually strives to perform at his best.

Success tip

'I use "key words" associated with my specific goals and deep breathing techniques to remain focussed in a game.'

Photo Courtesy of Tony Feder/Sporting Pix

The key points about relaxation are:

1 LETTING GO

It is a letting go of all effort—an effective strategy to relieve distress and tension and burning up energy unnecessarily.

2 A VARIETY OF TECHNIQUES

No single control strategy is effective all the time so you will need to utilise a variety of techniques.

3 REQUIRES PRACTICE

Like any skill, it requires practice and perseverance, but enormous rewards will come your way.

■ *Learn to be silent. Let your mind be quiet, listen and absorb.*

Stefan Edberg

The success of Swede tennis great Stefan Edberg is a remarkable story. After collecting in excess of $17 million in prize money and winning over thirty-six major tournaments, Edberg still remains an extremely positive and relaxed human being. Quiet and respectful, exceptionally determined and always in control of his emotions, Edberg allows nothing to disturb his concentration. With two Wimbledons, two US Opens and two Australian titles, Edberg's consistency at the highest level is outstanding. His daily commitment and professionalism reflects a life of self-discipline. Each morning he does 900 skips, 100 sit-ups, and 100 press-ups before breakfast and his tennis regime is planned meticulously. Edberg believes in, as much as possible, keeping life simple, remaining calm and unhurried.

Universally popular and respected, Edberg is the ultimate professional and role model of all that is good in sport.

WHAT RELAXATION CAN DO FOR YOU

There are two major groups of benefits that enhance your performance levels.

1 PHYSICAL BENEFITS

- **Energy or fitness benefits**

Relaxation enables you to conserve energy. Relaxed individuals often do their best work near the end of a day when their opponents are tiring.

- **General health benefits**

A regular relaxation schedule will lead to a healthier and happier self. You will eat and sleep better, and be ill less often. You will perform better, and generally feel more at ease with the world.

- **Illness benefits**

The maintenance and repair of the body is greatly enhanced with relaxation techniques.

2 MENTAL BENEFITS

Have you ever had a 'panic experience' during a day? You have perhaps recognised it when you have been suddenly called upon to say a few words to an audience. You know what can happen here. Being able to 'still' the mind and think objectively is a valuable asset in such situations.

Control of your mental processes is enhanced by your ability to relax in such pressure situations. Whether you 'choke' or remain as 'cool as a cucumber' depends upon this learned ability.

The ability to always be able to think clearly in all situations leads to:

- avoidance of panic
- regular occurrence of 'insights'—the right thing to do just pops into your head
- management of distraction

■ *Remember—it is not usually the situation that causes performers to worry, it is their reaction to the situation*

Clare Carney

Current Junior World Champion Triathlete, and younger sister to Emma (the current World Champion), Clare is immensely skilled, possesses boundless talent and unshakeable determination. Her motivation is to excel in her sport and she 'loves winning'. Whilst a relative new comer to triathlon racing, Carney's performances have been outstanding and reflect her unbelievable discipline. It is little wonder that Clare Carney remains ahead of the pack!

Success tip

'I can relax when I believe my mental preparation for a race has been thorough. I train hard, think about my pleasing performances and always believe in my ability to do very well.'

Photo Courtesy of Tony Feder/Sporting Pix

- enhancement of memory
- greater application of concentration
- higher levels of confidence.

In other words, you become 'mentally tough'.

RELAXATION TECHNIQUES

It is your responsibility to utilise the technique that works best for you! **Remember**: If at first you don't succeed, try something different.

<table>
<tr><td>

TIP

Never fall into the trap of some individuals who never stop to relax. Such people are like a woodcutter who never stops to sharpen his axe—he has to work harder to do what used to be easy.

</td></tr>
</table>

- **Sit or lie down in a quiet place, free from distractions**—take two or three calm, slow, deep breaths. Accentuate the outbreath (exhaling) and then pause for a moment after each breath is released and say to yourself: relax, calm, easy.

    Begin this technique with eyes open, then gradually let your eyelids close during the last slow breath. Feel yourself sink heavily (melt) into the seat and all muscles gradually relax.

    Actually concentrate on focussing your attention on your breathing rhythm—becoming more relaxed with each exhalation.

- **Take a brisk walk or some other exercise** (i.e. stretches, push ups, sit ups)—this will relax you and therefore enable a feeling of calm to be restored. Exercise provides the individual with an opportunity to channel tense, aggressive feelings into a socially acceptable behaviour. The other advantage of exercise is that it will increase stamina levels and enable you to cope more effectively with the demands of competition.

- **Imagining you are looking at a blackboard**—every time a thought enters your mind, see yourself wipe it clean. Whenever you feel stressful or anxious, write on your 'blackboard' a word or two that signifies what is causing the anxiety, then deliberately clean the blackboard again—see only blackness.

- **Relax your jaw**—when you feel hurried, inadequate, doubting your abilities or anxious about your achievement level, notice how tightly shut your jaw is. Consciously relax your jaw at these times. Try yawning—let your lower jaw drop!

- **Watch other high achievers**—monitor how they relax themselves; use them as models. Observe signs of tension; when you see such signs, quickly monitor your own situation, i.e. are your hands clenched, abdominal muscles held tight?

- **Close your eyes, imagine a pleasant scene or relive an enjoyable occasion**—allow your mind to drift into these past successes; feel the tension go.

- **Talk with your leader and/or trustworthy professionals**—gain the necessary reassurance and 'unload' unnecessary fears/anxiety.

- **Self-massage**—to relieve headaches, tired eyes or strain, use fingertips to find the tender spots in the neck, shoulders, forehead, temples—press and let go with circular movements.

■ *Whenever we are relaxed and calm, we are linked to our inner power and insight*

(Many more suggestions and relaxation techniques are listed in Chapter 12, 'Conquering stressful situations'.)

Mastery of these relaxation techniques will be enhanced if you:

- relax in the ideal environment, i.e. a quiet, warm, comfortable room.
- set aside a period of time (preferably between 10 and 20 minutes) daily to practise suitable techniques.

TENSION 'TIP OFF' LIST

How to tell when you are reaching your limit and needing to relax:

		Yes	No
1	Are you becoming more argumentative with your friends?	☐	☐
2	Do you require increasing quantities of sleep?	☐	☐
3	Do you have difficulty getting to sleep?	☐	☐
4	Are you often hungry all the time?	☐	☐
5	Do you suffer headaches, stomach aches, colds, infections etc.	☐	☐
6	Do you overdo one type of activity?	☐	☐
7	Are you withdrawing from friends?	☐	☐
8	Do you feel helpless?	☐	☐
9	Do you feel restless, anxious or worried?	☐	☐

If you answer 'Yes' commonly to the above questions realise that your coping system is heading towards **overload**.

YOUR ACHIEVEMENT TENSION LIST

Make two lists. In the first, list all the situations that cause you the greatest stress, worry and anxiety. On the other, list a few situations that you handled very well in the past, e.g. your best performances.

■ *Shut down now to avoid serious damage and get into relaxation*

Now repeat this procedure regularly.

- Using the relaxation exercise that suits you, get into a relaxed state of mind.
- Picture one of your best achievements and recall the pleasure of such relaxed and purposeful events.
- Now picture in your mind one of your stressful situations. Attempt to inject the pleasurable and confident feelings from your mental experiencing of your best achievement into this

stressful situation. That is, try and duplicate the calm, confident, pleasurable and successful atmosphere from one to the other.
- In this way you will conquer these stressful situations.

FOR THE LEADER

Poor achievement is more frequently a consequence of over-arousal than under-arousal. Often a leader will assume the opposite and partially contribute to the continuation of the problem by berating an individual to try harder, when intervening with specific strategies to calm the person down would be more beneficial.

By educating individuals to implement daily practical relaxation strategies, the likelihood of inappropriate levels of tension disrupting levels of performance will be reduced. Assisting them to quiet their bodies and minds will also enhance their self-confidence levels and ability to eliminate undesirable thoughts and feelings— **essential qualities for successful performance**.

DON'T FORGET

1 Relaxation brings with it insight.
2 Experiment with a variety of relaxation techniques—establish which methods work most effectively for you.
3 Relaxation is an excellent way to reduce the negative side effects of over arousal and conserves energy wastage.
4 Schedule time to stop. Resist the temptation to become active. Stop and free yourself long enough to listen and observe what is going on around you.
5 Utilise relaxation prior to visualisation and when planning new strategies—all the time!
6 Calm the body, clear the mind.

■ *Sometimes it's better to relax and gather your thoughts than to keep working harder*

WHAT SPECIFIC RELAXATION TECHNIQUE DO YOU UTILISE WHEN COMPETING?

■ *Know how to and when to relax*

NAME	SPORT	RESPONSE
Gary Neiwand	*Cycling*	Slow, deep controlled breathing. I sometimes imagine that I am in my 'ideal' place away from the pressures and demands of racing. I do not allow myself to be rushed.
Shelley Gorman	*Basketball*	Deep, slow breathing, focussing on specific muscles which are tense and relaxing them.

10 MOTIVATION
Internal motivation works best

Motivation is the desire, drive, hunger or stimulus for action and success. Highly motivated individuals are the ones who consistently achieve at a high level. It is absolutely vital, therefore, if you are serious about improving your performances and reaching new heights, that you should spend time understanding motivation, discovering what works best for you, and then use it. There are many motivational factors but the one that produces the best result is strong desire from within to achieve your goals and improve your success level.

WHAT WORKS

Successful people use a variety of factors to motivate themselves. A study of motivational factors reveals that some have the potential to provide greater, longer lasting benefits than others. Understanding motivation is therefore important. Find what works best for you and use it.

The successful individuals mentioned throughout this book, and who have conscripted their wisdom and experience, have revealed that the following factors have motivated them to strive and chase and work hard. After reading the rest of the chapter you will realise which of these factors produce the best results and should therefore be the ones favoured by you.

1   **BEING THE BEST**
Want to do my best
Be the best I can
Achieving goals
Love competing against self
Fulfil ability
Love being challenged
Reaching ambition
Big performance

2   **THINGS THAT INSPIRE**
Watching great individuals
Watching great events

3   **LOVE COMPETITION**
Compete against others
Dislike losing
Love the challenge

4   SUCCESS FILES

Of self and others
Videos
Scrap book
Mind games

5   SPURS

Prove to others
Failure and disappointment

■ *To be the best*
To beat my best
(PB)
To be the best of
the best (elite)

Michelle Fielke

Michelle Fielke is an incredible athlete with uncanny anticipation on a netball court. The goal defender/goal keeper plays for the Garville Club in South Australia and has represented her state at age group level since 1982 and open level since 1984. Fielke has captained the all-conquering World Champions since 1989 and has represented Australia at international level on 70 occasions.

Superbly fit, competitive by nature and one of the country's most consistent performers, Fielke dedicates herself to training and motivating those involved in netball throughout Australia. Her quick thinking and composure on court coupled with a professional attitude regarding getting the job done ensures that she is an excellent ambassador for this very popular sport.

Success tip

'I am motivated by an inner drive to succeed at the highest level. I love the challenge of competition and hate to be beaten. I strive for continual improvement in my game and still am driven by a burning desire to be the best I possibly can be.'

Photo Courtesy of Stuart Milligan/Sporting Pix

INTERNAL MOTIVATION WORKS BEST

So people can be motivated by a variety of factors. These factors fall into one of two broad categories—internal or external motivation.

Read the next two paragraphs carefully and find out which one works better for you.

1   INTERNAL MOTIVATION

This is the person's own internal desire to compete well. The most successful people fall into this category. They may find other motivations useful at times such as trophies, money or other people motivating them, but they do not rely on these. Just to compete for personal satisfaction and the love of achieving highly is itself a great motivating force for them.

Examples:
- Achieving personal goals
- Be the best they can.

2 EXTERNAL MOTIVATION

Whilst it is important that individuals receive recognition and some rewards for their endeavours, it is dangerous to participate in anything purely for such reasons.
Examples:
- Awards; bonuses
- Recognition from significant members of the community.

DEVELOPING INTERNAL MOTIVATION

Research shows that you will work harder and longer and will always want to excel at what you do if you can develop the internal factors of motivation.

Great satisfaction can be obtained by continually experiencing the thrill of achievement by working hard in a planned, progressive and determined way to overcome obstacles and accomplish challenging goals.

Mental skills, as outlined in this book, play a vital role in developing these intense internal factors.

It is important, therefore, that you set down a clear and progressive pathway to achievement and success as outlined in Chapter 5, 'Goals: A mighty motivator'.

FEAR AND DESIRE AS MOTIVATORS

Two powerful motivators dominate human behaviour but with opposite results—fear and desire.

Whilst **fear**, such as the fear of failure, drives many individuals, it can restrict, tighten and finally destroy them and their performance goals.

On the other hand, **desire** is a strong and positive force driving many other individuals with its openness, directness and ability to continually make achievement of goals possible.

So reduce the fear of failure and concentrate upon the potential of strong and consistent desire to bring you all the goals you have planned for yourself.

■ *It often takes just a little extra effort to be considered outstanding*

DEVELOPING INTERNAL MOTIVATION

Drop the word 'can't' and replace it with 'can' in your vocabulary.

Drop the work 'try' and replace it with 'will' in your vocabulary.

Focus all your attention and energy on the achievement of objectives you have set out for yourself.

List your strongest desires, write next to each the benefit to you of each, and regularly examine the list.

Talk regularly to those who have similar desires and are successful.

For every one of your desires, develop a simple, positive self-talk phrase or sentence and repeat it often (e.g. I will allow nothing to stop me).

Mentally experience the feeling of the achievement of each desire and do it often.

Concentrate with great intensity on the successful completion of anything you start.

Note: The importance of **realistic goal setting** (those stepping stones to success) is strongly linked to the development of your **internal motivation**.

Every person has a vital role to play in motivation. Always encourage others to excel at whatever they do—not for the glory they may receive, but rather for the satisfaction and sense of achievement they will experience by overcoming obstacles and accomplishing challenging goals.

> ■ *Motivation influences the quantity, quality and direction of behaviour*

The benefits of surrounding yourself with self-motivated individuals will be:

- a greater desire to work harder and for longer periods of time
- a greater likelihood of higher quality and quantity output
- fewer disruptions and interruptions (excuses) when completing assignments
- a happier, more settled and clearer approach towards others.

Keith and Ross Smith

The initiative and courage displayed by Australian aviators Keith and Ross Smith, who in 1919 became the first people to fly from London to Australia, is truly remarkable. Their aircraft, a 23 metre, 6 tonne First World War Vimy bomber, flew at 160 km/h and had an open cockpit. The Smith brothers accepted the challenge levelled at them by the then Australian Prime Minister, Billy Hughes, to complete the journey in less than 30 days and with only the clothes they were in, a razor and toothbrush each, they took off from Hounslow, England.

Weather conditions were appalling for most of the trip. Flying through Europe's bitter winter, their goggles clogged with snow and with the icy winds penetrating the open cockpit their sandwiches froze solid. Across the Middle East and Asia they endured searing heat and violent monsoonal storms. Undeterred, the Smith brothers pushed onwards without navigational equipment and through some of the world's most politically troubled areas.

Of the six crews that originally set out, some crashed, some vanished, others were imprisoned in Yugoslavia, or were attacked by desert brigands. Only the Smith brothers made it to Australia on time—a second plane limped home 9 months later!

The historic flight took 27 days. When the Smith brothers touched down in Darwin, the 19 000 kilometre epic of endurance was then the world's longest flight. Their reward was 10 000 pounds and a place in aviation history.

The initiative of Keith and Ross Smith served as the curtain-raiser for taking aerial travel out of the realm of fingers-crossed barnstorming into the age of great airlines. Their courage is now legendary and blazed the trail for today's international airlines and challenges us all to answer the question: Why be last when you can be **first**?

> ■ *Dare to be different, follow your dreams*

Photo Courtesy of Tony Feder/Sporting Pix

Cathy Freeman

Australia's best-known contemporary female athlete, Cathy Freeman, was the first Aboriginal athlete to represent Australia in an Olympic Games (Barcelona, 1992). She also became the first runner to win both the 200 m and 400 m sprint double at a Commonwealth Games (Canada, 1994) and she did both in Games record time.

Her success is just reward for continued discipline, an extraordinarily tough training program and a great fighting spirit. The lissom athlete with tigerish determination is a wonderful example for the Aboriginal community and at 21 years of age, Freeman could become one of Australia's greatest gold medal winners ever. Motivated by a desire to promote her Aboriginal people internationally, she is quickly developing into a potential world beater.

Success tip

'If you want something bad enough you can achieve it. I believe whoever wants to win the most, will. It comes down to who's the hungriest.'

DO'S AND DON'TS OF MOTIVATION

Don't:
- be negative
- threaten
- punish
- bribe.

Do:
- encourage
- support
- provide opportunities
- remain positive and clear.

THE BASIC NEEDS OF PEOPLE

All behaviour is need oriented. If you wish to assist individuals achieve their potential and remain motivated, address the following needs.

■ *Sarcasm never results in positive motivation*

1   FUN

Provide varied, challenging and enjoyable activities, which will not only maintain interest level but also enthusiasm. Attempt to design tasks that introduce creativity and spontaneity as well as reinforcing skills necessary for high achievement.

2   AFFILIATION

Surround yourself with people striving to achieve great things. To be with people who respect each other and share a common interest or goal reinforces identity and security.

3   COMPETENCE AND SELF-WORTH

Do whatever possible to protect individuals from losing self-worth and, more importantly, reinforce the positive abilities they possess. Encourage them to focus on their abilities, teach them to be optimistic and to tackle tasks that are difficult or challenging.

■ *Positive feedback, attention and approval will maintain motivation*

DON'T FORGET

1 The consistently successful individuals are usually intrinsically motivated, that is, they are motivated from within.
2 The motivated achievers have a burning desire to be the best and adopt a daily program that reflects this desire.
3 A leader can develop motivation within people by designing environments where achievement is emphasised and mutual encouragement fostered.
4 Individuals are usually motivated by a combination of intrinsic (internal) or extrinsic (external) factors.

MOTIVATING INDIVIDUALS

The following is a list of suggestions as to how leaders can develop the level of motivation in a positive manner. Tick which ideas you are willing to implement in the coming weeks.

1 Ensure that you are available to help others—never give the impression that you are too busy to talk, listen and offer advice if requested. ☐

2 Listen rather than talk. Check that what you have heard is what was said, then try to act on/rectify the concerns if possible. ☐

3 Always welcome, support and encourage; praise and reward initiative. ☐

4 Remain clear and logical at all times. Resist the urge to allow your emotions to blur what must be accomplished. ☐

5 Encourage honesty, respect any attempt to voice opinions and discuss issues of concern—always welcome feedback. ☐

6 Issue challenging goals and targets. Ensure everyone believes the goals can be achieved and create a healthy level of competition within everybody. ☐

7 Consciously display inspiration and initiative. Be totally positive and always generate hope—expect success. ☐

8 Create a variety of avenues through which people feel appreciated and valued. ☐

9 Assist individuals improve their PBs and to develop their skills further. ☐

10 Create an environment in which everyone can experience positive interactions and support for each other. ☐

11 MENTAL TOUGHNESS

If the mind is strong, you can achieve anything

Mental toughness is another common characteristic of consistent high achievers. Whilst some may be born tougher than others, it is a mental state that all can develop. It is the mental ability to persevere, of being unwavering in direction, of pushing on when everything seems against you and of fighting on no matter what the situation is. Mentally tough individuals always take things in their stride. They never allow circumstances to take control of them. Because they have developed mental strength, they are always in control.

MENTAL TOUGHNESS MEANS CONTROL

There are many situations that occur that have the potential to distress and upset individuals and restrict them from maximising their talents. Immeasurable combinations of uncontrollable variations exist, all capable of throwing very talented individuals off the road to success.

Consistent success demands that you control what you can, **and control your emotional response to those things not under your direct control**.

If you desire excellence, you must accept ultimate responsibility for controlling your emotional response to such factors.

■ *Control emotional reactions— remain focussed, unmoved and allow nothing to stand in your way*

■ *Be fearless, innovative and persevere*

> **Yiannis Kouros**
> Greek ultra marathoner Yiannis Kouros is 'mental toughness' personified. To run 1060 kilometres from Sydney to Melbourne in April 1987 in five and a half days on less than 6 hours sleep is a truly remarkable achievement—even more remarkable given the weather and road conditions, the traffic, the constant disruption of spectators etc. (all factors not directly controllable by him). Kouros claims that 70 per cent of the effort in any ultra marathon is mental and that he meditated, planned and concentrated solely on the run for two months before it even began. He always appeared composed, breathing in tempo and relaxed in his mind—a place he utilises to process positive thoughts and to express emotional controls. Here, indeed, was a performer completely in control—ultra marathon, ultra mentally tough.

■ *When you feel you can't go on, take one more step*

THE CHARACTERISTICS OF MENTALLY TOUGH INDIVIDUALS

1 **They give total 100 per cent commitment and effort.** They always try their hardest, give their all and are willing to take calculated risks in order to achieve success. After competing, they are usually exhausted but content in the knowledge that their effort was remarkable. **What about you? How would you rate?**

2 **They remain optimistic, positive and expect to achieve.** They possess tremendous inner reserves of strength and self-belief,

even in times of adversity. They are not shaken or disillusioned when a crisis occurs, but rather deliberately concentrate their thinking towards the challenges of change and gains to be made from such potentially negative problems. They appear unmoved when others start to question and doubt their capabilities and usually respond in a more determined manner to conquer any adverse situation. **How do you rate?**

■ *Refuse to entertain the possibility of failure—radiate an undefeatable attitude*

3 **They project a strong physical presence.** This is so particularly during a crisis when the odds are stacked against them—when their backs are to the wall. They have the capacity to demonstrate levels of endeavour and effort and execute their skills correctly when required. They dress impressively and always exhibit the qualities of a winner, regardless of the situation. **How do you rate?**

4 **They take total responsibility for monitoring and exhibiting pleasing achievement levels.** Mentally tough individuals are honest and will not offer excuses or look for scapegoats in order to explain a disappointing outcome. They make an honest assessment of what took place, implement a constructive action plan to minimise the likelihood of failure occurring again, and approach the next challenge with enthusiasm and vigour. **How do you rate?**

5 **They possess unwavering trust and belief in themselves, which saturates their thoughts and activities.** As mentioned in previous chapters, possessing a realistic and healthy opinion of yourself is a cornerstone for any consistently successful

individual. Without it, the individual will more than likely lack the dedication and sustained purpose necessary to overcome the obstacles to be overcome for victory. **How do you rate?**

Kathy Watt

Regarded by many as the toughest woman in sport, the 49 kg, 30-year-old Kathy Watt is both a Commonwealth and Olympic Games cycling champion. Incredibly talented and determined, Watt combines super fitness and endurance with enormous mental resolve to destroy the world's strongest competitors on the hills when they tire and begin to hurt. An outstanding athlete, capable of remaining focussed for long periods of time, Kathy Watt spends countless hours on the road training and is planning for further success in Atlanta (1996) and in Sydney (2000). Known as the 'Warragul Flyer' and regarded as potentially Australia's greatest ever cyclist, Watt pushes herself daily through pain barriers and believes there is nothing capable of stopping her from achieving whatever she wants from her sport.

Photo Courtesy of Tony Feder/Sporting Pix

The message being passed on by mentally tough individuals is:
- persist and never give up
- control what you can
- control your emotional response to those things not under your direct control.

HOW DO YOU RATE IN MENTAL TOUGHNESS?

The following questionnaire entitled 'Mental Fitness for Achievement' will test your level of mental fitness. It will help you ascertain what your strengths and weaknesses are and provide guidance for you to devise a plan of action to remedy the weaknesses.

■ *Remember— talent is extremely common, disciplined talent is very rare*

MENTAL FITNESS FOR ACHIEVEMENT

NAME: _____ DATE: _____

Rate yourself 1–5 for each of the following statements.
(Never 1; Seldom 2; Sometimes 3; Often 4; Always 5.)

1   I become totally absorbed in the challenge of improvement.

2   I am always very confident I will do well in whatever I undertake.

3   I have a clear, positive and realistic image of myself.

4   I regularly set challenging and specific goals.

5   I have a burning desire to improve my talents.

6   I employ specific relaxation and visualisation techniques.

7   I am able to keep trying even though fatigued.

8   I often think about achieving 'personal bests'.

9   I schedule regular times to imagine myself being successful and reaching my targets.

10   I evaluate each achievement and try to use failure as an opportunity to learn.

11   I can control my anxiety level.

12   I deliberately maintain positive thoughts throughout each day.

13   I actively remember and record my previous successes and relive how I felt on those occasions.

14   I remain self-confident in my abilities no matter what happens.

15   I see myself as a capable and successful person.

MIND AND BODY AS A TEAM

Increasingly, research is proving that high achievement levels reflect total mastery of both body and mind. Obviously the higher the level of skill and fitness, the greater control the individual has over his or her performance output. Therefore, individuals capable of recording personal bests and performing consistently well are those who have conditioned both their bodies and minds to form a reliable and successful combination—both work in harmony to produce rewarding outcomes.

Individuals who have demonstrated the ability to perform successfully universally agree that their experience is one characterised by complete control, an absence of fear and sufficient energy to perform their skills in a concise and automatic manner. In fact, such individuals usually sense a degree of wholeness between their physical (body) and mental (mind) aspects of performance.

Percy Cerutty

Percy Wells Cerutty was an Australian world famous coach of athletes in the 1950s and 1960s. He bore a reputation at home and abroad as a rude, irreverent anti-conformist who had absolute confidence in himself. He dedicated his life to mental and physical excellence and was no stranger to human toughness. Cerutty was a weak, sickly and underprivileged child. At age 7, he contracted a case of double pneumonia that caused partial paralysis of his left lung and any physical exercise caused severe discomfort. Nevertheless, Cerutty would display extraordinary will-power to continue to race even though he suffered chronic migraine headaches and was usually sick after the event.

At age 42, Cerutty suffered a nervous and physical breakdown and adopted a philosophy of 'strength through nature'. He rejected life in a city environment, took up marathon running and continually thrusted himself against pain. He deliberately pursued the reverse of comfort and by his mid-fifties Percy became a freelance coach.

Cerutty trained his athletes at Portsea sand-dunes. Feeding them mostly raw foods, he would push them continually through pain barriers claiming that 'you must suffer in order to succeed'. His camp was a back-to-nature haven where pain and sacrifice were endured in new ways, and the soft ways of urban living were forgotten.

Cerutty demanded total dedication from each runner and set a specific goal for each. He was only interested in achievement. Herb Elliott, world champion mile and 1500 metre runner stated that none of Cerutty's athletes could surpass Cerutty's will to win, competitiveness and determination. Cerutty was a talker and a doer and he would courageously perform almost frightening athletic feats. His successes were living triumphs of human spirit and will-power. Even till his death in 1975, Cerutty persisted with his rugged life philosophy and shortly before he died at age 80, Cerutty was stronger than when he embarked on his new life at age 43. In 23 years of coaching at Portsea, Cerutty coached 30 world record holders, and his philosophies raised horizons and pushed forward our conceptions of human limits.

It seems this ability to mentally detach oneself from the potential distractions of the immediate environment and move to a place that is conducive for consistent success is a major ingredient allowing such individuals to remain totally focussed and 'in tune' with their inner power.

■ *The tone of the body has much to do with the pace of the mind*

THE REWARDS

The rewards from developing mental toughness qualities are well described in the following extracts from the poem entitled 'if' by Rudyard Kipling.

1 The ability to keep your head when all about you are losing theirs—**always cool and calm in a crisis.**
2 The faith to trust yourself even when others are doubting you—**unwavering self-belief.**
3 The wisdom of patience and perseverance and to never give up—**commitment.**
4 The integrity of never dealing in lies—**always being honest.**
5 The sense of not appearing too wise—**never lose the common touch.**

> **TIP**
> Mentally tough individuals set daily a task that is challenging, difficult and often one that they do not particularly like. They tackle the task and persist until they have completed it. This is one way of nurturing the skills required by mentally tough individuals.

Greg Williams

Dual Brownlow Medallist (1986, 1994) and Best and Fairest (Geelong 1985, Carlton 1994), Greg Williams is very much propelled by ambition and self-pride. One of the most gifted and consistent performers in Australian rules football (he has represented his state on 8 occasions), Williams is always seeking to improve his skills, stamina and strength. His work ethic and willingness to do extra training to rectify deficiencies, coupled with his immense desire to be the best he can ensures that Williams remains amongst the truly elite players of the AFL.

Success tip

'Mental toughness to me is knowing I can do whatever is asked of me without ever doubting my abilities or allowing myself to be distracted from my task.

   I play best when I stick to my game plan and exercise self-discipline. I allow no one to stop me.'

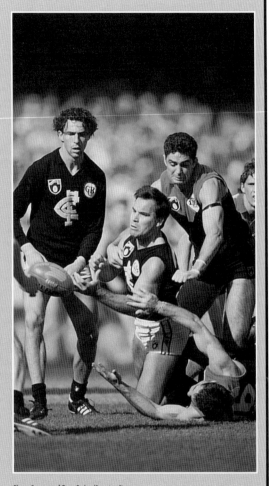

Photo Courtesy of Tony Feder/Sporting Pix

SELF-RESPONSIBILITY IS THE KEY

> **TIP**
>
> If you know of people who radiate the mentally tough qualities outlined here, arrange an opportunity to meet and discuss with them how they went about acquiring, practising and maintaining such crucial qualities.

Mental toughness is the pinnacle for any person. Without it they will more than likely simply achieve in a sporadic and inconsistent manner. The higher the level of competition, the greater the importance of employing the various elements of mental toughness spoken about in this chapter. Talent at elite level will rarely prove to be sufficient—the difference usually will be in the ability the person has in mastering and executing correctly the essential fundamentals of the task whilst remaining unmoved or undistracted by stress produced by the importance of the occasion.

   Like all mental skills discussed throughout this book, mental toughness can be acquired after a great deal of practice and perseverance. An individual can, by honestly evaluating and monitoring themselves, concentrate on specific factors that will lead to improvement and, ultimately, acquisition of these essential qualities. The key to improvement is the person again accepting **individual responsibility for directing their lives**.

WHAT SUCCESSFUL PEOPLE DO

Mentally tough individuals push on when everything seems against them and they fight on, no matter what the situation. They think on challenges and continually radiate optimism and enthusiasm. Rather than allowing circumstances to take control of them, such people confront situations of hardship or obstacles. They know that through self-discipline, self-sacrifice and industry they will achieve great things.

People renowned for their mental toughness appear free of fear and other self-imposed restrictions and have trained themselves to remain clear-headed and focussed at all times.

Their controlled, positive mental approach enables them to really come into their own when the going gets tough.

Such individuals recognise that 'if the mind is strong, nothing will stop them'.

Reflection

When we spend a minute reflecting on the sporting sensations of Australia's past, all universally radiated a fierce desire to win and a hatred of failing. The invincible 1500 metre runner Herb Elliott, the golden girl of athletics Betty Cuthbert, the tennis pair of Ken Rosewall and Lew Hoad, the freakish distance swimming of Murray Rose, the speedway racing great Jack Brabham, the coolness of golfing great Peter Thomson, the courage of world bantam weight boxing champion Jimmy Carruthers, the determination of Australia's greatest female swimmer Dawn Fraser or the fabulous middle distance runner John Landy—all these proud Australians achieved victories in outstanding fashion often against great odds and with the most primitive of preparations.

It was the actions of Australian champions like these that assisted their country emerge into better times after the Second World War. Their efforts inspired a nation, rekindled patriotic pride and helped focus the dreams of ordinary people on competing with and succeeding on the world stage.

DON'T FORGET

1 Live with purpose, to be the best you can be.
2 The key to consistent success demands that individuals control what they can, and control their emotional response to those things not under their direct control.
3 Mentally tough individuals remain optimistic, positive and expect to achieve, even in times of adversity. They hunger to be the best and are prepared to take the necessary steps to be successful.
4 Mentally tough people never give in.
5 Use powerful affirmations.
6 Perseverance remains the basic ingredient for anyone who wants to be successful.

■ *Be so strong that nothing distracts you from achieving your goals or disturbs your peace of mind*

Photo Courtesy of Norman Bailey/Sporting Pix

Anne Currie

The recently retired Anne Currie was Australia's number one amputee sportswoman. Her feats in the 100 metre and 200 metre freestyle and 4 x 50 metre freestyle events earnt her three world records. Currie claimed four medals in the 1992 Barcelona Paralympics.

Born without legs and with only three fingers on her right hand, Currie thrilled the world with her determination to be successful in her sport.

Her courage and dedication gained her international recognition and her triumphs remain one of the most inspirational achievements by any athlete of the modern era.

Success tip
'If you want to achieve great things in life, be prepared to make sacrifices, set goals and realise that your accomplishments will usually reflect how hard you have worked. If you want to be the best, you've got to put everything into it.'

CAN YOU EXPLAIN WHAT THE TERM 'MENTAL TOUGHNESS' MEANS TO YOU AND HOW DO YOU DEVELOP IT WITHIN YOUR SPORT?

NAME	SPORT	RESPONSE
Stephen Moneghetti	*Athletics*	The ability to withstand and sustain extraordinary levels of physical pain and exhaustion. It is developed by being very dedicated and hard on myself regarding a daily commitment to training and goals.
Gary Pert	*Australian Rules Football*	The ability to be unwavering in direction, through 'ups and downs', to push self beyond limits.

12 CONQUERING STRESSFUL SITUATIONS
Calm the body, clear the mind

Stress occurs when there is a major difference between what you believe is being demanded of you, and what you believe your capabilities are, and when you believe the outcome to be very important. The key to the situation is to alter the deep concern with which you view the situation and its outcome. Your perception of it needs to be changed and this will reduce the stress.

Stress has robbed more people of energy, victory and enjoyment than any other factor. Stress can destroy self-confidence by making individuals believe that they are incompetent. It can also deny them the pleasure of demonstrating the skills they have mastered. It causes interpersonal conflict, induces illness and drives some people to early retirement. But it can be conquered.

The term 'stress' is associated with distress, meaning any kind of demand, burden, pressure or hardship. When people talk about feeling under pressure or stressed, they are referring to their inability to cope satisfactorily with how they see the demands of a specific situation. This leaves them feeling threatened, worried, tense and frustrated. It is important to point out that every situation is potentially dangerous and every individual responds accordingly.

The good news is that all people can learn to handle stressful situations. You can learn how to recognise stress and how to manage it to your own advantage.

HOW TOO MUCH STRESS AFFECTS YOU

It is when a person feels that a situation is too daunting or too frightening that performance output will most likely suffer and the body tenses to negate clarity of thoughts and efficient usage of skill (**flee** response).

When a situation is believed to be manageable or challenging, the person will utilise the adrenalin and additional energy levels to meet and defeat the situation (**fight** response).

■ *Realise the problem is more in the mind than in the occasion. It is what the individual imagines will occur, the harm or fear the occasion will present. The key to controlling stress is altering perception—what you believe is being asked of you.*

Photo Courtesy of Tony Feder/Sporting Pix

Shelley Gorman

'Whenever feeling stressed, I try to relax the tension in my shoulders by taking slow, deep breaths. I find that if I am well prepared (physically and mentally) before each game it is much easier to control my emotions and if I do become negative in my thinking, I deliberately make an extra effort to do the small things correctly.

I aim for consistency, composure and confidence on court, particularly under pressure, as I find this teaches me mental toughness. I always have short-term goals and believe these help my confidence and ability to cope with whatever situation I find myself in on court.'

THE KEY TO STRESS MANAGEMENT IS RECOGNISING THE SYMPTOMS OF TOO MUCH STRESS

The following table entitled 'Your State of Stress' illustrates the various negative effects that a high level of stress may have on a person.

YOUR STATE OF STRESS

Which of the following symptoms concern you? Tick the box if you think the symptom contributes to a lack of control on your part during the day.

1 Psychological
- Feeling overwhelmed; expression of self-doubt ☐
- Inability to think clearly or logically ☐
- Unable to concentrate; easily distracted ☐
- Not feeling in control; vulnerable; defensive ☐
- Narrowing of attention — not aware of alternatives ☐
   — poor judgements ☐

2 Physiological
- Increased levels in:

— Heart rate	☐	— Adrenalin	☐
— Blood pressure	☐	— Flushed face	☐
— Sweating	☐	— Sweating palms	☐
— Respiration	☐	— Frequent urination	☐
— Muscle tension	☐		

3 Behavioural

• Rapid talking	☐	• Trembling	☐
• Foot tapping	☐	• Increased blinking	☐
• Muscle twitching	☐	• Broken voice	☐
• Pacing	☐	• Easily upset	☐

PRACTICAL METHODS OF REDUCING THE NEGATIVE EFFECTS OF STRESS

When you are highly stressed, you may fail to focus attention on appropriate cues, misdirect your anger and become increasingly negative and critical towards yourself and others. In this situation, you must maintain composure, relax and think clearly and logically in order to accomplish your targets.

The following is a list of practical suggestions that will alleviate (reduce) the negative effects of stress. Mark some of the strategies that appeal to you and try to adopt them.

Remember, it is your responsibility to become aware of your own stress levels and recognise what situations causes you most anxiety. Try to manage it to your advantage.

- **Smile and laugh**. Exhibit calm, confidence and positive expectation. Welcome and greet people, e.g. 'It's good to see you'.
- **Listen to soothing music**. Seek stillness, quiet and peace.
- **Consciously monitor your breathing patterns**. Slower deep breathing will lessen anxiety. Hold your breath for 10 seconds then exhale, letting go of all tension. Focus on a trigger word, e.g. calm, relax, control, winner, victory, peace, unbeatable. This will minimise energy wastage. Inhaling—strength and vitality. Exhaling—ridding body of old, unwanted air, anxiety and worry.
- **A period (5–15 minutes) of quiet time**. Uninterrupted, private time will enable you to 'focus' on your own performance.
- **Lying down or sitting with your back straight**. Take two or three deep breaths, exhaling slowly and concentrating on 'seeing yourself' performing successfully. This form of relaxation will enable improved performance as it increases the amount of oxygen in the blood.
- **Slow down the speed of your speech**. Speak in a soft, soothing tone.
- **Engage in some light physical activity**. Stretching, brisk walking, jogging and other physical movement in itself often releases tension and anxiety.
- **Remove all caffeine, alcohol and drugs from your diet.**
- **Practise making friends (via mental rehearsal) with distractions and the factors that may cause you to be anxious.** Adopt an aggressive or assertive approach to the situation. This also reinforces your capability to cope, manage and conquer potentially stressful situations. This is both affirmative and positive.
- **Restrict negative or distracting influences, such as noise, from interfering with your concentration.**
- **Speak confidently and encouragingly to others.** Develop an atmosphere of friendship, 'team' and mutual support for a common cause. Enter every occasion without giving any thought to defeat. Concentrate on your strengths instead of problems.
- **Study various meaningful sentences or quotes.** Choose those that (if used with visual imagery) highlight your positive strengths and qualities.
- **Monitor your own self-talk and negative thoughts.** Concentrate on previous success and maintain positive thoughts. Reject negative—I can't! Inject positive—I can.
- **Work hard at reducing the negative consequences associated with such important occasions.** Emphasise what you expect to happen positively rather than negatively.

■ *WARNING*
If you are feeling highly stressed, tell someone **today**.

■ *Don't give in until you get help*

Make stress work for you:
— I can   — We can
— I will   — We will
— Just watch me!   — Just watch us!

- **Consider how to reply to the question: 'What is the worst thing that could happen to me now?'.**
- **Construct a positive environment prior to the event—secure, friendly and reliable.**

THE RESULTS OF STRESS MANAGEMENT

With appropriate utilisation of the various techniques outlined, you will be more able to maintain a moderate (optimum) emotional arousal level, which will ensure a greater possibility of:
- a clear mind and thinking patterns
- appropriate utilisation of skills and responses
- adequate motivation and drive to achieve personal goals and targets.

Photo Courtesy of Tony Feder/Sporting Pix

Lindsay Gaze

Coach of the Melbourne Tigers in the NBL, Lindsay Gaze has been the force of Australian basketball for more than 30 years. His dedication and commitment to basketball in Australia is outstanding, and without doubt, as the fastest growing sport in the nation, basketball owes an enormous debt to him.

Gaze believes that to be successful in basketball you must be an enthusiastic trainer, desire to be the best and appreciate the impact appropriate mental training/preparation has upon performance.

Success tip
'I deliberately attempt to minimise the importance of the game and have trained myself to remain calm and composed to reduce my stress level.'

MEASURING YOUR OWN STRESS LEVEL

Complete the following questionnaire relating to your own stress level and at the conclusion, answer the following questions:

1 What did I learn about myself?
2 What could I do to reduce the effects of stress in my life-style? List specific strategies.

STRESS QUESTIONNAIRE

NAME: _____ **DATE:** _____

Instructions

Tick the following statements that relate to your usual behaviour.

Do you:

1 Have a habit of explosively accentuating various key words in ordinary speech? ☐
2 Always move, walk and eat rapidly? ☐
3 Feel impatient with the rate with which things are done? ☐
4 Frequently attempt to do a multitude of things simultaneously? ☐
5 Have difficulty concentrating when listening to another? ☐
6 Experience a problem talking about issues that are bothering you? ☐
7 Feel guilty when you relax and do absolutely nothing? ☐
8 Find yourself getting angry or agitated easily? ☐
9 Have little time to spare to enjoy the things you do? ☐
10 Maintain a well-balanced and healthy diet? ☐
11 Have a hatred of failure and have difficulty accepting it? ☐
12 Get queasy in your stomach, or stiff neck and shoulders, during the day? ☐
13 Feel generally uptight and tense? ☐
14 Have difficulty in your working relationship with your administrators? ☐
15 Take home work to complete it? ☐
16 Think badly of yourself for not meeting demands of the job? ☐
17 Experience headaches? ☐
18 Use an effective method of managing stress (i.e. exercise, relaxation techniques) ☐
19 Feel powerless to solve problems? ☐
20 Complain to others often? ☐

Gary Neiwand

Australian cyclist Gary Neiwand won his third consecutive sprint cycling gold medal at the 1994 Commonwealth Games in Victoria, Canada. His gold medal achievement was all the more outstanding as he had to overcome a knee injury only two weeks before the Games. Rather than putting pressure on himself or worrying about the restrictive nature of the injury, he deliberately rode in Canada to enjoy himself and to do his best—he brought home **gold**!

Success tip

'Successful performers know where they are heading and have specific plans to focus on along the way. It is my experience that they love achieving and have unwavering confidence in their ability and display a professional attitude in all they do.'

Photo Courtesy of Bob Thomas/Sporting Pix

Jennifer Capriati

The excessive emotional demands of competing in elite sport were highlighted in May 1994 when the teenage tennis star Jennifer Capriati was arrested on a marijuana charge. A celebrity at age 13, her life on the tennis circuit was often lonely, friendless and depressing. Her problems were compounded by her parents' unrealistic expectation that if she didn't win, it meant she was a loser. She felt she was only likeable as a person if she was winning!

Sadly, Jennifer Capriati, tennis phenomenon and Olympic Gold Medallist in 1992 had a total lack of emotional support and balance in her life-style. She needed someone who would love her for who she really was rather than feel judged according to her tennis ability. Her story is a reminder that all that glitters is not gold! And of the dangers of living a distorted, stressful and very public life-style.

Whenever trying to
solve a problem:
- Collect information
  about it.
- Break the problem
  down into smaller,
  more manageable
  parts.
- Tackle the task step
  by step.
- Believe you will
  solve the problem
  successfully.
- Get to it—take
  action!

DON'T FORGET

1. Stress has much to do with perception. The key in controlling stress is altering perception—what you believe is being asked of you.
2. When under stress, an individual experiences physiological, psychological and behavioural changes.
3. There are many different ways to relieve stress levels. It is imperative that the person utilise the techniques that work best for them—**practice is essential**.
4. You can be a stress carrier or stress reducer. Encourage, smile and quietly support others and always exhibit calmness in a crisis.
5. You create a role model for others, so don't panic. Adopt an attitude of no matter what happens, it can be handled.
6. It is usual that every problem contains within it the seeds of its own solution.

The journey of life takes us through many times of success and failure, happiness and sadness. We remember the happy and successful times as the most enriching experiences of all. Although the stressful and disappointing times do not appear outwardly to benefit us, they are in reality the times that build strength and character in us all.

13 SUCCESSFUL LEADERSHIP
Educate for independence, not dependence

> *CREED OF A LEADER*
>
> *To lead people, walk behind them.*
> *As for the best leaders,*
> *people do not notice their existence.*
> *The next best, the people honour and praise.*
> *The next, people fear.*
> *And the next, people hate.*
> *When the best leader's work is done, people say:*
> *'We did it ourselves!'*
>
> Lao Tse

LEADERSHIP QUALITIES

Think of a leader you admire, it is probable that they exhibit most of the following qualities.

1 RESPECT OF SELF AND OTHERS

- Not quick to judge or dismiss another's viewpoint.
- Does not pretend to be someone other than who he or she is.
- Demonstrates high regard for others.

2 ABILITY TO WITHSTAND CRITICISM AND PRESSURE

- Remains calm, clear and controlled in a crisis.
- Will not criticise people publicly.
- Refuses to 'lash out' at external factors, i.e. press, officials.

■ *Those who take too many shortcuts end up going around in circles*

3 ALWAYS POSITIVE AND ENCOURAGING

- Smiles often.
- Genuinely welcoming.
- Optimistic and energetic.

4 SENSITIVE LISTENER

- Provides accurate feedback.
- Maintains eye contact; approachable body posture.
- Does not interrupt.

5 A HEALTHY SELF-IMAGE

- Enjoys a laugh—particularly at self.
- Participates in a variety of physical activities.
- Attempts to 'balance' daily stresses.

Photo Courtesy of Tony Feder/Sporting Pix

Stephen Kernahan

Made Captain of the Carlton Football Club in 1986, after only 22 senior games at 22 years of age, Stephen Kernahan is a veteran of 10 seasons in the AFL and has played in excess of 200 games. He is an inspirational leader, brilliant goal kicker and excellent role model for younger players. Kernahan has won the Best and Fairest award on three occasions (1987, 1989, 1992), has been named All Australian Player five times (1985, 1986, 1988, 1992, 1994) and has participated in 12 State of Origin games. His supreme aerial ability, strength and capacity to seize the initiative in crucial games has made him one of the champions of the AFL.

Success tip
'I try to set an example to others in what I say and do. Rather than say too much to other players, I prefer to let my actions "on field" do the talking.'

Jill McIntosh

Quiet achiever Jill McIntosh is noted for her calmness under fire. Professional, honest and forthright, she is meticulous in her approach and considered a 'listening coach and very much team-oriented' in her strategies. The Canberra-based national netball coach takes her sport very seriously, handles pressure very well and shows no signs of worry or stress.

Success tip

'From my experience, to be successful at elite level you must have a determination to develop your skills to the maximum, be committed to hard work and radiate positivity and enthusiasm at all times.'

Photo Courtesy of Tony Feder/Netball Australia

6 ENTERTAINS NEW IDEAS/INNOVATIVE

- Will take calculated risks.
- Always willing to learn, i.e. desire to improve/increase knowledge.
- Attempts novel training, and marketing, sales strategies/ methods.

7 CLEAR IN VISION

- Radiates self-belief—strong leadership and commitment.
- Unwavering—'tunnel-like'.
- Will not allow factors to detract from achieving overall goal.
- Ability to enthuse and inspire others.

8 A HIGH MORAL CODE

- Disciplined, loyal and honest.
- Willing to admit errors/mistakes.

9 THOROUGHLY PREPARED

- Leaves nothing to chance—well organised and punctual.
- Evaluates alternative strategies.
- Searches for 'winning edge'.

10 ENCOURAGES INDEPENDENCE/SELF-ASSESSMENT

- Stresses individual responsibility and monitoring of own achievement levels.

11 EFFECTIVE COMMUNICATION

- Perceptive; responds to individual needs.
- Articulate—brief; to the point.
- Utilises a variety of results, e.g. video, handouts, diagrams, speakers—non-verbal, visual, verbal.
- Encourages interaction.

12 ABILITY TO EXTRACT MAXIMUM EFFORT FROM INDIVIDUALS

- Ability to motivate individuals in competitive situations.
- Knows how to 'tap into' each person.
- Knows when to be democratic or authoritarian in approach.

13 KNOWLEDGE OF THE FUNDAMENTALS REQUIRED FOR SUCCESS WITHIN THE FIELD

- Possesses accurate and up-to-date information.
- Advice is based on a sound appreciation of the talents and skills required.
- Ability to diagnose faults and prescribes appropriate corrective measures.

LEADERSHIP AND YOU

Before you establish your individual style of leadership, reflect upon the unique experiences and talents you bring to your leadership position. Make a list of your strengths and weaknesses and

Paul Wade

Thirty-three-year-old Socceroo Captain Paul Wade has 'carved out' an extremely distinguished career with a game plan based around his 'never say die' attitude. He has played more games for Australia at international level (in excess of 70) than anyone else and always has acted as a diplomat and loyal servant for soccer throughout the world.

Wade prides himself on his consistency, aggression and hard work. Despite two major ankle operations he is still driven by his desire to play soccer at the highest level and demonstrates an attitude to winning that continues to motivate those around him.

Success tip

'Leaders require inner confidence, unending determination and the capacity to focus automatically on the crucial aspects of the game.'

Photo Courtesy of John Daniels/Sporting Pix

ascertain which aspects of your leadership require ongoing attention. What type of leader do you really want to be? Why?

Think of the leaders you do not respect. Why is this? It is vital that you avoid adopting any of the traits of leaders you find objectionable.

Remember: You are the role model for others and they will always look to you for guidance, approval and appropriate behaviour. Ensure you provide an excellent model for them.

One of the most important qualities of leaders is the courage to do what is right.

■ *There is no right way to do a wrong thing*

EVALUATING YOUR LEADERSHIP EFFECTIVENESS

How effective are your leadership behaviours? Complete the following questionnaire, which should highlight areas requiring improvement and reflect your honest assessment of leadership ability.

SUCCESSFUL LEADER'S CHECK-LIST

NAME:_____ DATE:_____

Instructions
For each of the following categories give yourself a rating and a case study.

Categories	Definition	Assessment (1 = weak; 10 = strong)	Case examples (action phase)
Open thinking	• Challenges old ideas and traditional thinking • Quickly identifies key issues in complex problems • Open to others' suggestions		
Emphasis on 'action'	• Looks to the future, and seeks opportunities • Challenged by risks and difficulties • Anticipates problems and is forward thinking		
Knows what makes others tick	• Takes time to understand people; gets to know their standpoint, their needs and concerns • Knows how to motivate • Encourages others to talk and express themselves		

continued over

Concern for impact	• Considers impact of action on others • Builds respect and trust for actions		
Self-confidence	• Confident of ability, will take on challenge and accept responsibility for success or failure		
Assisting and developing	• Sets realistic targets, gives clear feedback, monitors progress and provides support		
Building team success	• Encourages joint decisions and problem solving • Anticipates and resolves conflict and gives clear roles		
Motivating	• Knows what motivates individuals and uses this to get the best out of people • Varies style and mode of encouragement		
Reaching others	• Provides information and makes plans clear • Paints a clear and imaginative picture		
Sharing achievement	• Communicates clearly and frequently • Shares vision; shares success		

NEVER UNDERESTIMATE THE POWER OF PRAISE

Leaders must attempt to satisfy the following psychological needs of individuals in their charge.

1 **Opportunity to achieve**—to develop oneself and master personal goals.
2 **Security**—to feel comfortable and trusted in a non-threatening environment.
3 **To belong**—to feel a member of a friendly, worthwhile and supportive group; to be valued and appreciated.
4 **Independence**—encouragement of individuality, initiative and the freedom to pursue these traits.

It is unlikely that any long-term or consistent achievement or success will be gained from your leadership unless these four fundamental needs of your people are satisfied.

NUTURING THE NEEDS

Practical examples of how you, as leader, can create and maintain an atmosphere amongst individuals which will nurture the satisfaction and fulfilment of these psychological needs are as follows:

1 Encourage smart, clearly identifiable dress, i.e. uniform (unity).
2 Provide competitive and challenging tasks/goals/targets (achievement of goals).
3 Immediately defuse contentious issues (maintain security).
4 Invite suggestions and opinions, encourage participation in decision making (belonging, opportunity to achieve).
5 Actively promote their proud history (i.e. achievements) and proposed future directions.
6 Display loyalty and open support for others (security, trust).
7 Stress success and accomplishment of personal best targets (achievement).

A leader will be successful if they have the ability to satisfy the varied needs and expectations of individuals and assist them to achieve realistic targets in a well-organised environment. Leaders should always be approachable and diplomatic.

> ■ *Do unto others as you would have done to you!*

West Coast Eagles
AFL Premiers in 1994, the West Coast Eagles seem set to power through the 1990s with their brand of tough, relentless and disciplined football. Since 1990, the Eagles have appeared in three Grand Finals and their record reflects the vision, dedication and thorough preparation their leader and dual premiership coach, Michael Malthouse, brings to each performance. He heads a very professional, highly skilled unit and is exceptionally knowledgeable on opponents, hard working and an uncompromising person who demands total commitment to team goals and tactics at all times.

ENHANCING ACHIEVEMENT

The following is a list of ways a leader can actively influence an individual's self-esteem and likelihood of success.

1 Minimise failure and emphasise success. Encourage people to make an honest assessment of what went wrong, emphasise what can be learnt from the situations and implement a specific plan of action to remove the likelihood of such errors occurring again.
2 Ask individuals to take an active interest in the formulation and planning of policies. Opportunities to contribute at meetings should be encouraged.
3 Teach individuals to evaluate their own progress and establish a support network where everyone assists each other—young and old, experienced and inexperienced.

> ■ *Courtesy costs nothing yet it conveys much*

4 Delegate authority to others and carry out surveys of needs.
5 Organise gatherings where people (across different age groups) attend and interact.
6 Never belittle, ridicule or humiliate individuals publicly. Endeavour to provide constructive advice and develop an atmosphere where people feel safe.

Research indicates people function best and grow in an environment of action. Complete the following table by listing specific ways you can create a successful environment for achievement.

1 Genuine participation and team-work.	_____ _____
2 Mutual respect for individual needs.	_____ _____
3 High performance expectancies and standards.	_____ _____
4 Prompt, constructive feedback.	_____ _____
5 Appropriate incentives and rewards.	_____ _____
6 Loyalty, commitment and enthusiasm.	_____ _____

SHARE THE LEADERSHIP ROLES

Increasingly, successful leaders are acknowledging the need for having a professional, reliable and supportive infrastructure of talented assistants. This is not to say that the leader hasn't the capabilities to be consistently successful but sharing the workload may enable the leader to enjoy the role more and work more efficiently as a result.

Advantages of appointing talented individuals to positions of responsibility include:
1 Provides you, as leader, with greater freedom and flexibility in time management.
2 Encourages shared responsibility and ownership of challenges.
3 Generates new ideas, strategies, perspectives.
4 Facilitates greater likelihood of communication amongst team members. Some individuals experience difficulty approaching the leader yet will happily discuss issues with assistants.
5 Provide a trustworthy, sensitive confidant role for the leader.

To ensure maximum likelihood of gaining the most from people, surround yourself with outstanding and honest individuals and utilise their insights and enthusiasm. Recognise the contributions that individuals make and provide positive feedback regularly so that everyone experiences your appreciation and respect for their efforts.

FEEDBACK

Successful leaders recognise that ongoing feedback is essential if individuals and teams are to maintain their effectiveness. Giving feedback is often easier than receiving feedback. The following are some practical guidelines on how best to give and receive feedback.

GIVING FEEDBACK

1 Be specific rather than general.
2 Focus on the behaviour rather than on the person.
3 Avoid overloading with advice. Provide a few suggestions at a time and a possible strategy for their achievement.
4 Share information about what you saw or heard.
5 Look for the necessary cues to ensure when someone wants to listen to your feedback.
6 Encourage clarification of what was discussed.
7 Remember to provide positive feedback as well as feedback that may be viewed as critical yet constructive.

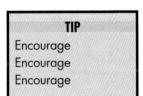

TIP
Encourage
Encourage
Encourage

RECEIVING FEEDBACK

1 Do not interrupt and maintain attention on what is being said. Allow yourself to hear what is being suggested without judgement.
2 Welcome feedback as an opportunity to collect data that will improve your performance even further.
3 After feedback has been given, seek clarification of any points if you feel it will be valuable to you.
4 Avoid arguing about the accuracy or validity of the feedback now—give yourself time to digest what was said.
5 Acknowledge and thank the person for providing honest feedback to you.

WHAT MAKES A SUCCESSFUL LEADER?

Are successful leaders born or made? Undoubtedly, such leaders possess enormous stores of determination and drive—usually they are high achievers since childhood!

Successful leaders tend to radiate an attitude of singlemindedness and pursue their dreams with an unstoppable passion.

Above all, what makes a leader successful is their ability to get up and strive again and again, despite disappointments and setbacks, and to adhere to the goals they set themselves. They believe in setting the example by maintaining consistency in performance and always seek to attain personal bests.

So the challenge for each individual is to develop their leadership potential and to improve at a faster rate than their opponents. Successful leadership requires innovation, self-discipline and total focus on remaining 'number one'.

Have you got what it takes to meet the requirements of successful leadership?

DO WE HAVE AS MUCH SENSE AS A GOOSE?

Next time you see geese heading to warmer climes for the winter flying along in a 'V' formation, you might be interested in knowing what science has discovered about why they fly that way. It has been learned that as each bird flaps its wings, it creates an uplift for the bird immediately following. By flying in a 'V' formation the whole flock adds at least 71 per cent greater flying range than if each bird flew on its own. *People who share a common direction and sense of community can get where they are going quicker and easier, because they are travelling on the thrust of one another*.

Whenever a goose falls out of formation, it suddenly feels the drag and resistance of trying to go it alone, and quickly gets back into formation to take advantage of the lifting power of the bird immediately in front. *If we have as much sense as a goose, we will stay in formation with those who are headed in the same way we are going*. When the lead goose gets tired, it rotates back in the wing and another goose flies point. *It pays to take turns doing hard jobs—both with people or with geese flying to warmer climes*.

The geese honk from behind to encourage those up front to keep up their speed. *What do we say when we 'honk' from behind?* Finally, when a goose gets sick, or is wounded by gun shot and falls out, two geese fall out of formation and follow it down to help and protect it. They stay with it until it is either able to fly or until it is dead, and then they launch out on their own or with another formation to catch up with their group. *If we have the sense of a goose we will stand by each other like this!*

Together
Everyone
Achieves
More

DON'T FORGET

1 As a leader, you set the standard for others. As their role model, encourage them to aim high.
2 Recognise that everyone is a potential achiever—even if they may be disguised as a failure.
3 A successful philosophy of leadership reads: person first, winning second.
4 Leaders must display honesty and the courage to do what is right.
5 Always be willing to listen, learn and implement new ideas and concepts.
6 Encourage, encourage, encourage.
7 When people believe you have faith in their ability, they rarely let you down.

■ Getting to the top will always involve elements of great risk, a willingness to persevere and a capacity to work hard, even against great odds!

All successes are intertwined with setbacks. Often the decisions you make may not be right all the time either. However, you must press on with even greater resolve.

Fulfilling your dreams will require great amounts of energy and courage. Maintain your commitment, passion and focus and allow nothing and no one to stop you as you climb **to the top**.

Remember: What you accomplish in life is ultimately **your responsibility**.

Anthony Stewart has also published a book entitled *SECRETS OF SUCCESS*, which is a celebration of the achievements of Australians in sport. The book provides an insight into the lives and performances of 50 successful Australians, including heroes of yesteryear such as Dawn Fraser, Sir Donald Bradman, Ron Barassi, Sir Jack Brabham and Ron Clarke, through to modern-day stars such as Dennis Lillee, Jeff Fenech, Greg Norman, Debbie Flintoff-King, Allan Border and Andrew Gaze.

This attractively presented 128-page, hard-bound publication examines the ten common characteristics exhibited by all sporting champions—qualities that can be applied to sport, business and education.

Great for corporate or individual gifts, personal motivation and recognition awards, *SECRETS OF SUCCESS* can be obtained by sending your name and address plus a cheque for $23.00 per copy (including postage) to

PERSONAL BEST PTY LTD
PO Box 47
Tally Ho Vic 3149.

Anthony Stewart is also available to speak at corporate and sporting functions. Contact (03) 9887 7220.